Spirit Walks
with
Gregory

Spirit Walks with Gregory

Mick Avery

Transcribed and Edited by

Sylvie Avery

Published by Spirit Teaching™, California, U.S.A

Spirit Walks with Gregory
by Mick Avery

Published by:
SPIRIT TEACHING™, Ltd.
18340 Sonoma Highway
Sonoma, California 95476
www.spirit-teaching.com
(707) 939 9212
(888) 746 6697

All rights reserved. No part of this book may be reproduced or transmitted in any form or by any means electronic or mechanical, including photocopying, recording or by any information storage and retrieval system, without written permission from the author, except for inclusion of brief quotations in a review.

Mick and Sylvie Avery assert their right under applicable law to be identified as the authors of this work.

Copyright © 2005 Mick and Sylvie Avery
First Edition
Printed in the United States of America

Publisher's Cataloging-in-Publication

Haye, Gregory (Spirit)
 Spirit walks with Gregory / [channeled by] Mick Avery ; transcribed and edited by Sylvie Avery.
 p.cm.
 LCCN 2004107344
 ISBN 0-9755599-1-5
  1. Spirit writings. 2. Spiritualism--United States. 3. Mediums--United States. I. Avery, Mick. I II. Avery, Sylvie. III. Title.

BF1301.H349 2004   133.9'3
                              QB104-700246

Gracious and Infinite Spirit
Help us to walk the path of sincerity
That we may share the wisdom
And love you bring
May these insights not linger
And waste upon our lips
For this right is not ours to keep
May we prove with deep humility
The existence of the spirit
And the continuity of life
As you guide our footsteps
Through the gates of our destiny
Safe in the arms of love

Sylvie

Acknowledgements

It would be impossible to mention all of those who have been supportive to us whilst writing this title, whether it was helpful practical advice or by an encouraging word at the right time.

Special thanks must go to Robyn, who's literary skills have once again been called upon and even despite a busy lifestyle of her own has managed to tactfully deliver helpful suggestions of the work in progress, which has been so invaluable.

To John, Ann, Nicki, Liz and Caroline, for their love and for being there for us and of course, our spirit friends, who have entrusted us with their beautiful teachings, of which we are honored to deliver on their behalf.

Our appreciation also goes to Simon Warwick-Smith and Cierra Trenery for their guidance in the publication of this book.

Table of Contents

Introduction	5
About the Medium	7
Gregory Haye and the White Cloud Group	9

WALKS

Harmony Through Meditation	13
Perception	19
Growing	23
Finding The Ladder of life	27
Free Will	33
No Time for God	39
Crossroads	41
Certainty	47
Parallels	49
Power and Control	51
Life's Decisions	57
Exploitation	63
Letting Go	67
Where There Is a Will	71
Conflict of Thought and Racism	75
Lies	79
Do Not Leave Negativity to Chance	83
Dreams Not Nightmares	87
Be Yourself	91
Just Do Your Best	95
Positive Harmonic Propulsion	99
Values and Your Planet	103
Responsibilities	107
Understanding Affliction	113
Changing Your Inner Vision	117
The Power of Prayer	123
Checks and Balances	129

A Question of Access	133
Vibration	137
Protection	141
Structure of Thought	143
Knowing Yourself	147
Grieving and Negativity	151
Truth or Consequence	157
Allowing Dysfunction	161
Healing Ring of Light	165
Love	167
Clarity	173
Relationships	179
Sleep and Your Astral Body	183
Respecting Other People's Views	189
When Our Worlds Meet	193
Materialism Will Hold You Back	197
Your Choice	201
Interpretation is Everything	205
You Are Your Own Angel	211
Ghosts	217
Poltergeist	221
Do Not Be an Island	225
Just an Observation	229
Effort	233
The Importance of Forgiveness	237
The Importance of Words and Language	241
Religion and Reincarnation	245
Christmas	251
Sitting and Frustration	255
Guide Hierarchy	259
Spirit and Other Life	263
For Those Walking the Spirit Path	267
The Keys	271
Meditation – The Master Key	273

Introduction

This second book by Gregory Haye continues the stance of greater thought enabling the reader to understand the connection between their spirit and the world on which they live.

Individuals sometimes tend to believe that only those who are aware of their gifts of insight can understand such subjects and so fail to identify their right of access to their true pathway. This tendency is extended to the perception of how anyone may bring about a real and lasting change for themselves, through this or any other like doorway and this in itself creates a vacuum in front of it.

Knowledge is to share, and this book serves to show how self-improvement can actually change our thoughts and perspectives into something both real and positive, for the good of all. With setting down the path of right thought, giving everyone a way to see and put aside the pain and fear they carry within, it shows how they may embrace a better vision of life, not just for themselves, but for those to follow.

This is a step-inducing book to bring about awareness of self in a real day-to-day manner, in simple though not condescending ways that the reader can grasp. Through his desire to help us, Gregory, the spirit guide, expresses his observations with humility, hopefully to bring the reader out of the habit of impoverishment of the mind. How we focus and observe turned into a mirror so we are able to see our thought and action for what it really is, so we can grow.

By discovering the spirit within each of us, the spirit that we are, we attune our senses to our higher mind and raise our vibration, which in turn will alter the way in how we see, think, and feel. Through meditation (or going within), we discover and come into contact with the real essence of who we are and allow this aspect of our nature to come to the fore, to illuminate our pathway with higher intent and harmony.

With practice, we can connect to our spirit to guide us, with purer thoughts and meaning. We all have this facility because we are all spirit. We are just having a human experience now. Investigate for yourselves. Once again, here within this book are the signposts to look for.

The Medium

Mick Avery was born in London, England, in 1952 and lives with his wife Sylvie, who is also a spirit medium. Music played a large part in Mick's early life; he was a musician and worked as an audio technician.

There had been situations throughout these earlier years when he had looked upon other forms of religious understanding, having an enquiring mind he was interested in establishing why we existed at all. When he met Sylvie, she introduced him to the concept of spirit and he later began his spiritual development. It felt like home!

It became apparent that Mick had an incredible gift as a deep trance medium, and because he had very little knowledge of spiritual philosophy, it was obvious that the words spoken through him when in this altered state were not his. They have not been taken from his sub-conscious memory either, so that was a bonus really. The effort he put into his development was consistent and continued to build, leading to a greater momentum within this field of communication, and his ability to become more mentally disconnected from the event whilst in 'spirit control' grew.

There have been and still are, many other entities who use Mick as a channel, but it wasn't long before Gregory Haye, the main spirit communicator, introduced himself and outlined the very specific work ahead. He wanted all of the subsequent sittings to be tape-recorded and transcribed for the purpose of publication.

Having extremely low self-esteem and even a slight stammer, Mick was somewhat overwhelmed by the trust instilled in him by spirit and although never for one minute doubting the integrity of Gregory, at times, he felt it to be a huge responsibility. However, Gregory has assured Mick and Sylvie that their spiritual work must never feel like a burden, but remains their freewill and pathway.

It actually turned out later that he and Gregory had arranged to meet up and do this work whilst in the spirit realms, before Mick's earthly journey began; however, Mick was unaware of this until Gregory told us of it. He used to see spirit when he was a child, but had gradually lost it as he grew up. He has never thought of himself as anything other than just an ordinary person and at the time was just as surprised at the unfolding events, but always a willing vehicle for spirit.

Now a gifted trance voice medium, Mick can go into the deep trance-state enabling spirit to communicate with us without the hindrance of his mind and thoughts getting in the way. Spirit temporarily take control of his body and his consciousness, enabling the personality, in this case Gregory Haye, to use it as a vehicle of expression. When Mick has returned from this altered state, he is unaware of anything that has just happened and has to listen to the recordings to understand these communications himself.

His mediumship is now finely tuned and he presents trance demonstrations to the public all over the world, and audiences are invited to put questions to Gregory on many diverse topics and in a perfectly natural way. Mick is also an accomplished trance healer, where a wonderful Chinese guide called Li Teow Sonicha, works through him to give healing to both people and animals.

Gregory Haye and the White Cloud Group

Who is Gregory Haye? We are all touched at times by those who inspire us, whether those who do so are here having this physical experience, or from the spirit world. Gregory is a remarkable individual who has brought much communication from the White Cloud Group, of which he is the main spokesperson. Gregory had his earthly existence in the early eighteenth century, being born in 1705 and lived near the village of Swaffham, in Norfolk, England.

He was an only child, and by the time he was three, his French mother Alicia, had already passed to spirit with consumption and so he spent the rest of his life with his father John Haye, an agricultural laborer. Eventually, he turned to help him when he was old enough and added his young strength to make a meager existence, working on a small strip of land.

Later, he was fortunate to be taken under the wings of Benedictine monks, who made periodic visits at the ruin of a local priory. It was from them that he received some very basic education and found his love of writing poetry, giving him a small window to express his inner thoughts and emotions.

He was to have a short hard life, as one rain-soaked night in mid November 1723, at just eighteen and a half years old, before he was able to realize any ambition he might have had, he was run over by a coach and horses and killed. Gregory was buried near to the grounds of Castle Acre Priory, in Norfolk.

Since his physical passing, Gregory has chosen to serve others, and one way he does this, within the spirit realms, is to help those who have recently passed over onto the next step of their journey. He shows them how to come to terms in their new environment and make progress within their understanding.

Another part of this service, or act of giving, is for him to communicate to us on the earth plane, via Mick, his instrument. He does this in order to share the benefits of knowledge, wisdom, and insights he has gained since his crossing over. This is not from an elevated position, but a different one as he sees it. He too is inspired and helped by the many enlightened spirit individuals of the White Cloud Group, who work with him in this constant quest to bring uplifting thoughts and visions of a world in which we may all share in peace and harmony.

Gregory has said of the arrangement, that he comes to speak on behalf of those minds of clear thinking, of the sentient energy that make up the White Cloud Group. They consist of many hundreds of individuals, all from various soul groups, who were brought together to educate and to instill the loving vibration of harmony and union throughout our world and the universe. They are here to bring about a greater awareness of the truths of all life, of what has been and what is to come, to help us to see where we are going wrong and how we may all help each other. The simple fundamental acts of giving and showing love, encouraging positivity, and in taking responsibility for our actions are vital for eradicating fear in our lives. They feel that in showing us the truth about ourselves in this way and what happens after our transition to spirit, is crucial for our progress. The need to control our thoughts and actions, and how discovering the 'spirit that we are' is the key.

In respect of this involvement, he explains how, in the spirit realms, he has found it very necessary to build up the scant education he had previously acquired in order to keep abreast with contemporary English language, particularly the modern idiom. In his distinctive soft voice, he shares his teachings and answers our questions in a gentle, modest, non-judgmental, compassionate, and frequently humorous manner.

There will be many books by Gregory and the White Cloud Group, including those by healing guide Li Teow Sonicha, and also Silver Fox, an Apsaroke Crow Native American. They will have varying formats and content, which, if the reader would like to follow, will gradually progress towards a high level of illumination regarding our evolution as a species, other realms of existence and so much more. We hope there will be no stone left unturned in our search for the answers to what life is really all about.

Harmony through Meditation

Events, scenes, and pictures dominate the planet on which you live, the place you live and each moment you live it. As you gaze in awe at the majesty and beauty of your surroundings, it can make you feel so small, for it is so perfect. The mountains, the trees, the flowers, butterflies, and birds ... everything you see is so perfect.

However, it is only thus because it is in harmony. It lives, all of it linked arm in arm, gently bathed in its own light and the energy of spirit, the energy of the eternal life force that flows through everything. To deny it and say it is empty would be to deny yourself. Therefore, you gaze upon this perfect panorama before you and you can feel so small, insignificant even, in wonderment of its sublime quality.

Friends, each one of you plays an integral part to its service and make up. You are all just as beautiful, just as perfect if you wish it – if you can just be. There is no difference between the scene before you and yourself, for if you can be in that harmony and balance with the aspect of God within you, acknowledging who and what you are and with all that surrounds you, then you will share everything that God is.

You are just a different combination. You belong at this time, at this moment, where you are, and you belong there because of your circumstances, because your life has brought you to this place. If you wish to go forward then be at peace with what you are, and if you do not like what you see, change it. It is all down to your wish and to your desire to improve yourself.

There are so many different modes of harmony you can express, sense, and witness. Harmony between yourself, the earth, and the spirit world that surrounds you, and very importantly, a harmony with your fellow spirit travelers, whoever they may be. The very fact that you have come to the point whereby you read these words, means perhaps that you are searching to make yourself more aware of the harmony that surrounds you.

It is not right that you should go through life and not experience harmony. Not experience truth or light, but to fall to the depths that disharmony and negativity can take you. It will take a great effort from your side and ours to bring about positive thought upon your plane of existence, because at this time it is trapped in a field of negative energy and needs to be dragged forwards to positive thought.

The harmony you feel wherever you walk, whether in your present existence or whether on our side in the spirit light, is so important. How you feel travels very far. You can strike a chord in one plane and it can lead to harmonic distortion in another. Harmony is something that you have to be very careful of and with, for if you are not careful and you upset it, it can set off a chain of events that take a long time to settle.

It is possible to change it from within, for through meditation, you can change how you think and how you feel. You may then tap into your higher consciousness, whereby you will become more connected with that stream of awareness and intuitively know on a deeper level, whether something is right or not. All of this recognition goes towards helping you to achieve a harmonic balance between yourself the spirit, the planet, and others whom you share it with.

When you meditate (or go within) you will notice how peace invades your mind, as if to try to show you what inner calm there can be. As if to express what this moment of peace may deliver to you. How this tranquility may cast adrift your fears. In this sublime richness, the unnerved hand of peace removes the furrows from your brow and lets your mind ascend and descend all in one go, all in one movement. Your vibration heightens in the stillness that surrounds and becomes you.

As you move within this experience and you become aware of what you are deep within, this tranquility is in harmony with your senses. Senses you had not previously been aware of. They have illuminated your mind to what you the spirit wishes you to see, and the peace is so great that it generates a welling-up of love within you.

This is not some idle chat to wile away many hours of darkness. By exposing yourself to beautiful things, you may take in those thoughts, which alight upon the mind, whilst at the same time becoming as one with the nature of the world around you.

If you came to a place untouched by human hand, a place of only nature spirits, where harmony breathes within and without, you would then be looking upon the perfect expression of life.

So how may you fit in with that expression?
How may you become a part of that?

To blend with a tree. How can you do that so well as the creatures of the wood, almost unseen, yet you know they are there?

Well, if you were in harmony with their world, they would not run away from you. If you were in real harmony with a fellow creature of a different race, it would not fear you; it would relax in your fine company. It might even communicate posture and be happy knowing that its life is not threatened – knowing that all is well and at peace – in knowing your light is there, and that you shine also.

The more you sit in meditation the more focused you will be, for as you become in touch with your spirit, the more presence of mind you will have. You will gain a new confidence in your approach and this recognition of your spirit self will become attractive to others.

Having this presence of mind of spirit is not difficult to achieve you just have to practice. You will find it is amazing how people will change once they are in touch with their spirit. How learning and many steps forward will transform one's personality into a more caring, focused and loving being. This is not something you wear as make-up that you take off at the end of the day, but with help and guidance, it will become a change in your personality.

Love and cherish all things, all moments of your life, so those times of tribulation may seem as leaves afloat, borne by gentle wind and may disappear. Love can be so bountiful – peace so comforting and it can be endless. Friends, you may find yourself there, letting the harmony within and the harmony without, link blissfully entwined upon your shore of life – the calm waters forever within your reach.

Cast your energy
In the purest form you are able
So you may become a part
Of the higher harmony field
That you may become aware
Of the purity and vitality of love
To bring rise to your spirit
And let you bathe in God's light

These castles
Are not disappearing images
They are mirrored only
By the purity of what we see
They are the scenery and sense
Of the greatest aspect of the universe
That we are all a part of
And significant in our meaning

Perception

Your perception of your reality is dependent upon how lucid your mind is. How accurate your recall. How well you store the information received and whether its sources are accurate or not. So really, how you view your reality is all a matter of question, whereby you find that you have to verify certain facets of it daily with others.

When you feel something is amiss or witness a strange occurrence, you may say: "Well look at that, have you ever seen anything quite like that?"

If the answer is: "Oh yes, as a matter of fact I have." You think, 'that's alright then!'

Only, how you view the world is very often how your next-door neighbor does not, and they may actually see something completely different. Therefore, we can go even wider, in that your perceptions will depend not only upon your existing reality, but also on how you feel. Whether you are negative or positive can turn your past views and ideas completely the other way around.

This is actually quite an amazing event. That what you perceive plays such an important part in your life, and what you perceive is only one side of the hub of your mind, if you like. It is how you gather your pieces of information. Like the colors in a picture brought together and laid out before you, for you to identify who you are. At least, with whom you think you are.

Therefore, bearing this in mind that you can be so liquid and unsteady in how you recall events, how do you think this may affect your view concerning the planet on which you live? The more we can get you to think about how you perceive a matter, the more you may begin to understand that the mind can change a lot. Each event as it unfolds before you may change your opinion, for nothing is fixed and nothing is final.

You may be between five and six feet off the ground, and if you look down there are your feet and above you are the stars. Well, that is a certainty – but even that is temporary, for you may be on a moving object; a bicycle, a motor car, a horse, and your whole perception and reality of experience is altered. So you must be careful not to assimilate all there is in life as being what is possible for you to experience.

If you think about it, to begin with, only a few men went up in an airplane and only a few souls had ridden in a motor car. Many people were frightened of them saying that it could not be done, and yet now, it is a commonplace event. Not one to inspire awe, on the contrary, it is something that is just taken for granted, like almost everything else. It is your way of life. It has become an integrated structure of life.

We then come to the next part of it, which is that of exploring the reality of your spirit. You may have encounters with the spirit within and discover that those ideas and scenarios you had previously conceived, were in fact, also unfounded. Consequently, I say to you, that as with science and technology, your mind and your spirit push forward and the more capable you are of recognizing new realities,

Perception

of perceiving yourself in a different light. You are capable of reinventing yourself because there is someone within, but that someone is at present attached to the physical, and that someone cannot be given up too lightly. You must make yourself known to you, so that you are looking at the right photograph, so you are taking part in the moving picture that you are, or you could become a ghost on the film.

You see, your perception of how you exist is very important, as it is one of the prime factors of engaging in positivity. If you perceive you are nothing, if you see that your life is somewhere near zero, then what you perceive of your own volition is of poor quality, little value or worse.

You can see why it is that when people get depressed they have to write out lists of what they find good or bad about themselves. One list may well be longer than another because it entirely depends upon the negative or positive forces within.

As we have discussed, by using your mind you can change your whole outlook and your whole perception of your world. That is not to say this is a false perception, it is just another way of looking at it. In reality, you have not changed anything either way. You have merely changed in how you view it. The results will be in your conscious and subconscious mind and how it relates to you as a character, how it sits with you and with your life. Thoughts that make you feel worthy, wanted and loved.

You only have to think it true and you can then get affirmation through reality, through seeing it there in front of you, as plain as day. This is achievable upon every level of thought or feeling, your perception and your reality can be brought together into one single thing ... your life!

The many fragrances of love come
When we give shelter to understanding
They are the mirror we all have
The gift where we may see
The true treasure within us
By content of the feelings
We may have
For one another

Growing

At times, you might think you do not walk your walk straight enough, that you do not look around the right corners or watch the sunset from the right spot at the end of each day. It is quite possible you will find yourself always challenging every move you make.

"Oh, am I doing the right thing?" "Am I thinking the right thought?" "If I think this, will it lead to that or not?"

You make your world very complex. You seem to have to find many different ways in which to take one-step forward, for there is a possibility you may step backwards, and that would never do. The constraints you put upon yourself and upon your lives are really quite awesome from our point of view. Restriction upon restriction you place there, like being bound hand and foot, gagged, blindfolded, and with earplugs too, possibly. Quietening your senses so that they are not too loud so they do not interfere too much.

Of course, I am taking this example to an extreme degree in describing the worst-case scenario. Because you as individuals, you as spirit who walk your earth who are having a human experience at this time, are all capable of looking much further. You are all destined for greater things, from the one who already thinks he has it all, to the one who has nothing. From the child who plays football in the street, to the individual who is regarded as the lowest of the low. All of you have room for change and growth. All of you can come forward, but you cling on to your old ways like rusty railings; you are not handcuffed to them and yet you remain there.

Well, the truth is often very difficult to take, for it means that you have to realize and acknowledge the many falsehoods and lies previously been given to you, possibly throughout your life, and it is very hard to do. Moreover, my friend, it is hard to grow … for that is what it is. You may say that this is just my opinion, but it is hard for me to understand how you can remain upon the way you are going, upon the treadmill that you are forever encircling yourselves with, without understanding simple, basic truths that may help you on your journey.

No matter how young or old you are, however much you think you know, let us help you. It is not that you are dreaming, neither is it a wish come true. It is real enough and if you take the trouble to look yourself, you will find that what I say is true. You have a spirit within – a separate entity to your physical body and it is not touched by the thing you call death. When your physical body is cast off, you are free once again.

It is a plain and simple truth that you have been given often enough maybe, but it seems that few listen….

"That truth's a bit frightening, a bit scary; we'd better not go that way!"

It has almost become a culture of negativity really, and what has to happen is a change around, a turning point must be reached in everyone's life. You must all come to an understanding of how the universe works 'to you.' Of how the truth speaks out to you and how the negatives can enlist your help in their quest for domination, if you let them.

You have such a seesaw life. One minute you travel along a road and everything is fine and you are reasonably happy, but you still know that in the back of your mind there is something missing. In addition, it does not matter how many pints of beer or bottles of whiskey you drink, there is still somehow a yearning inside you. There is a hole to be filled, which seems to be able to take any amount of things that are thrown into it. It is still there, a gnawing gap within your being.

You can fill it with love ... you can give yourself upliftment by discovering the bare facts of who you are, by discovering the essential you, so you may acknowledge you.

It may seem strange to say, but do you wish yourself 'good morning' when you wake up? "Oh hello, how are you today, it is so nice to see you?"

It is so much better than looking in the mirror and wishing you were younger or wishing you were older, but wishing you were not in the niche that you are. "Oh, woe is me!"

To all of you, you only have to look to find what is there. Do not take any notice of those around you who say you are crazy or pathetic, because you would wish to find out who you are and not what it says in books, magazines, or fast films on fast television. See 'you' when you look in the mirror. Look to see your spirit glow like firelight – gentle, full of possibilities, bringing you closer and closer to harmony, balance, and love.

There has never been such a love as this
That exists among the stars
That a place upon all things
You see how marvelous you are
Release your mind let it go free
Let it circle round about
All things must come eventually

All things will duly pass
Sweet songs all meant for thee
All gracious, all mighty
Spread those thoughts you have of me
Lay them out upon your throne
For I am not the one you lost
As you will see when you come home

Finding
The Ladder of Life

There are those on your planet who have much anger about themselves and about how others may influence their lives. People are kept in poverty. In bad housing, with lack of food, warmth, and clothing, and so as you struggle with your daily life it builds much resentment and negativity. The big billboard posters always showing a brighter shinier car – a girl with thick lips and a dazzling smile; inferring that if you have this much money, you can have all these things.

It is in situations like this that may drive people to robbery and violence. A feeling of utter worthlessness when these material effects are not achievable. Many in their walk of life may have nothing and no goals, because they are just not on the right playing field. They feel they are in the wilderness; they are walking blindly and aimlessly, and for many this becomes such a mental anguish. Such a torture, because they have not achieved the success the world was advertising. This then produces disharmony, anger, resentment, and lack of function.

The problem is that for many people on your side of life, if they do not have what they perceive they want in order to make them happy, they may even decide that it is never going to happen and take their own life – commit suicide.

It can drive many over the brink. I am not slating them nor being judgmental about their actions, but just simply saying how sad it is that someone has to go that far and then become a silent voice. How is it that we can get ourselves into such a mess?

It happens all the time does it not, for some fight all of their lives and get nowhere. It is like trying to climb up a steep muddy bank without having a good grip. Or a good life in this case, and despite the efforts of all of those around them, reason slips by and they fail. Just like calling out to life and only hearing an echo back, or so they believe.

Friends, those of you who may contemplate such a move, I know you are not doing it lightly, and see it as a way and means of how you may relieve yourself from this dilemma. Truly, there are ways of moving forward and this is not one of them. Except it is your choice, and nothing is held against you, your life is your life whatever you choose to do with it.

It is possible that you could live in a place and feel fear all around you. In any area, doubt, darkness, and an entire feeling of gloom can actually transpire from the fabric of the buildings right through to the people who live in them. In addition to this, the very fact of their collective ambience, the whole feeling and gravity of such a place, can bring one to their knees. Therefore, this may be the plight of those not living in areas of outstanding natural beauty my friends, but of merely bricks and mortar. The longer this is left to go on the more negative bugs it will gather, until you have nothing but a nest of bugs. Mankind has to be careful with social planning.

Imagine how someone who lives in such a place may feel when he or she ventures out into the countryside – like being on an alien landscape. It will certainly feel very differently from the rest of you. There seems to be an attitude of, 'well they've always lived there.' Yet, you would not treat cattle in the same way. At least you give them a green field to stand and graze in, a place where they may share life with the buttercups and flowers, trees and birds. At least that is something.

What is this teaching us? It is that man has to gain the respect of each other and the environment. You cannot just push and shove, insisting that people live in a place where you would not.

Now, this is all very well, I hear you saying – very idyllic, but not reality. Well, maybe not my friend, but you have to have a thought at least. You have to have an inkling of an idea as to where you may go from here, how you may achieve some kind of balance, for you clearly cannot stay as you are. There has to be some letting up – some help for those who cannot help themselves. Hindsight is not good enough after the event.

You must plan for the future and not be so entrenched in the past. Enrich your lives with progress. Make your life worthy of the spirit that you are, and of being remembered for good.

Yes, perhaps you have increased the standard of living (and I am not advocating a particular political point of view, I am merely stating a fact) but you have to have a balance within your society. You have techniques with which you may serve to heal people in your world, with medicines and operations, but your need is greater than you perceive at this moment in time.

Fine, if you are willing to pay for it, and that is just merely a small facet of the rift between people. It is all right for those who have, but for those who have not, they are separated from the rest of you. You have to understand that one of the main things in your life is to share.

There are many people who are lonely, who live in such a solitary manner, who are not wishing to be, but are forced to nonetheless. People who have no contact even though they may be surrounded by millions of others. All of this loneliness and deprivation needs to be noticed and addressed. They need to be gathered in, so they may gain a greater understanding of how they may find the ladder of their life. For some, it is just like trying to climb out of a swamp. A near impossible task it may seem, as the forces of negativity constantly suck them down.

There is so much work to do and so much upliftment can be experienced, for at least most of you can read a bit, and those of you who have hearing can hear. Therefore, the spoken and written word my friends, is the first and most important point of contact, but it has to be accessible and it has to be sharp and in focus, so that everything may be understood. It has to flow, so that every word and syllable makes sense, lights the mind, and fills or increases the yearning for more.

Alas, at this time, the have not's far outweigh the haves, and this will increase friends. I am sorry to say that the gulf will continue to increase, until somebody says: "Stop, I want to get off!"

It is the same all over your planet, from country to country, hemisphere to hemisphere, as you are now finding out.

It is our desire to fulfill our dream, to walk our walk with you. As we have said before, it can sometimes only take one word, one hand of comfort, and sometimes it may not work at all. It is each individual's choice of free will to take it or not, and it is a matter of whether they are ready to understand what is being given.

May love and light always walk with you, always be in your step, and always wear your smile.

We recognize all truth
As a valid point
All entity striving
For further understanding
How mind may expand
To accept new awareness
And take another step
Along the road to recovery

Free Will

For a very long time, man has sat around campfires and listened to stories from the elders, and because such people were older and wiser, there was a searching among their fellows for the knowledge that they possessed. These older folk had gained much wisdom and enlightenment through many years of traveling, along with much sorrow and pain upon their journey.

What followed was that many who were older began to think of themselves as different. Not necessarily superior, but more so that they counted for something, because they had lived to an old age so therefore, should be respected. Perhaps they had struggled throughout their life not being respected, and gradually had to gain respect through many trials over many years.

It was from the younger people that this respect was gained. Until a time when someone decided that old people are stupid and senile, are too detached from the reality that surrounds them or from the way things have moved forward.

It then comes about that someone younger than the old wizened one begins to talk sense also, and so they fall into a pattern. Gradually, as all the old people of the village become older still, they just talk among themselves about the various observations they make upon village life that surrounds them, for that is all they can really do now. They cannot go about their daily business for they have none. All they can do is to sit and philosophize about what they have learnt through their lifetime ... the old days!

Therefore, it seems there is a gap. A void between the generations who had previously lived in harmony and it is considered that the older ones cannot keep up with the new technologies. Well, that may be the case, but they do not have to be derided for it, for they may have so many lessons within them through which the younger people might learn. This is not to say you should always do what elder's say, for everyone can be wrong. Just because a person has lived on the planet for many years, it does not mean you must be unquestioning.

In young people, there is such a struggle for learning, because they feel they have to compete, in order to survive in the big bad world outside. Consequently, rather than in choosing what they would like to do, it becomes more like a competition, pressurized by peers, parents, and society.

On the one hand, you have an education system that tries to be of the highest quality, and fighting in between. Within this system, there will be groups of wealthy parents who can afford to pay for certain privileges, such as good schools, and because of their peer pressure, their children move into the circles that their fathers would expect. In fact, these are the only ones they would entertain, for they wish to make sure that their standing is maintained, and that they acquire a bright mind.

Of course, there is nothing wrong with a bright mind. It is necessary and healthy, but is not an absolute! Yes, you need to move onward and upward on your journey of life, to be able to accept understandings, but you do not have to be a genius to do that. You just have to be able to work out the simple mechanics of the mind.

You do not have to have super-intelligence to be wise and this can be an accumulative process over many years. You can be as 'thick as a plank,' as they say, and still have a very happy life my friend.

At the other end of the spectrum, there are numerous poverty-stricken places where there is very little schooling. Children are running around in the streets making their own games with little or no learning of written work and study. Their classroom is the street. These people come from totally different walks of life from the other group I have described, and through their life journey, they may change.

It is not to say that one journey may be more fruitful or better than the other. They may both be just as fruitful for their mind and have involved just as much learning, which could be equally crucial to that mind and their spirit.

You might have older people within your community who are still quite sharp. They may have some balance of the mind left and they may still speak wise words and have an open mind. However, one of life's processes can be that the mind becomes closed and self-centered.

"Listen to me, because I am older." Can sometimes be more like: "Listen to me, because I am hollow like a bell!"

You see, because of the structure of systems on your planet, people feel they are being 'told' constantly. That you all have a leader and you must all follow them around like sheep.

Maybe it is your desire to be a sheep, and that is fine if that is what you wish. Perhaps it could be dangerous not being a sheep in a particular country in which you live, depending upon the particular persuasion. Therefore, when speaking on matters of your plane, you have all of these variations and possibilities, but one thing stands out – you appear to clamor for guidance. You always seem to be searching for that higher mind within your midst. You know, the one who may be super-intelligent. Who must be highly regarded and then whose words must be followed faithfully. Consequently, because of this it generates more power for that person, whether you think they are correct or not, that is what happens.

Then you have little groups of people, all with their leader, and those leaders get together and form yet another leader, and they all do what they do and whatever they are told. It is how your systems are built up. You have all of this underpinning of power from one stage to another, and there is little individual freedom left.

One of the things the street kid works out for him or herself is that they are free spirits, for they have nobody to answer to, but themselves. Unfortunately, this can very often turn to anger and violence, for they have been excluded from their community or they become less and less within the eyes of those peers around them. They just feel left out and so unhappy with who they are, because they do not have a big house and a shiny car. As a result, this way can be equally as damaging.

The older ones within your community do have some very important things to say, and it is wise to listen to the wise. It is also wise to make your own judgment, for you have not lived their life and you do not necessarily see everything through their eyes, or they through yours. Life is all about a matter of opinion ... your own!

You do not have to follow each other like sheep, for you all have free will and you can make a success of the life you have. Bear in mind that everyone comes from a slightly different angle, a slightly different point of view, so you cannot follow each other around.

You cannot say: "He did that, so I will too." Because the effects upon that person's journey could be completely different from yours, it could have a very different effect and result upon your life.

I am just trying to make the point that your mind is your own. You have your own agenda, your own purpose. With peace and serenity in your heart and mind you may travel along your journey open to wisdom and learning, and not coating yourself with a hard shell that prevents you from growth.

Do not restrict yourself to the flock; it does not have to be that way, for you are as individual as every blade of grass is individual. Each one picked and studied will have a slightly altered state to it. Each seagull that you look at is faintly different. They all have slightly different markings that are not easy to see at first glance, but if you look very carefully, you can see the difference.

Try not to confine yourselves, in that you have landed on a spot on an island, and because you have made your nest there, that now there is nowhere else you can go. Well, a nest can be rebuilt. It does not have to be fixed to a post; it can be made mobile, in various forms depending upon your wants and needs. Fine, if you are happy with what you have, then you stick at it, but if you do find unhappiness creeping in, you may have become bored with your life and bored with the things you do. Realize that perhaps you are not the person you thought you were, that you have moved on – and it is perfectly okay.

It takes one thought
To make right
Those actions of evil
It takes just one mind
To think it

It takes one eye
To see it
As love comes over the hill
And just one ear
To hear the sovereign words
Of majesty and understanding

It breaks one heart
To see the foul ways
We may stand
On each other in dishonor
It takes one step
Upon the road of freedom

It can seem like a mile
To break the pattern
That was set in stone
But takes one breath
To say sorry
And one hand
To show peace has come

No Time for God

Do you see, you have a certain set of absolutes? That when you wake in the morning and open your eyes the sun is going to be there, even though it is sometimes covered by clouds. It will pass overhead across the heavens and sink to the other side, and the moon and the stars shall all do this with alarming regularity, for that is the pattern of it.

All manner of things upon your planet are repetitive patterns. Many of these pass right over your head and you do not even give them a second thought, as day-to-day you plummet in and out of ritual. You speak and communicate, eat, think, and use your physical body for the necessities of life. All that effort going into living – all that incoming mail to your mind, and yet, you have no time for God.

You have no time to experience who you really are.

My friends, if you gave one tenth of the time that you spent eating or bathing, thinking of how the source of life relates to you, think how possibly in touch you might become throughout your life. With just a little connection necessary to wake you up into what is real.

Perhaps it is the connotations of the three-lettered word. That it instills fear and entrapment. That it conjures up the associated feelings of indoctrination, icons, and religion. God is not an almighty being to be falling on your knees for or to lay prostrate on the ground for. Neither is it a deity or something so awesome that you must shield your eyes from.

No, there is God within all of you, behind that little doorway of inner peace, and you can just go there whenever you wish. It is there waiting for you – as you are waiting for you, and that may be the hardest decision you will ever have to make.

"Can I go there and see who I am?" "Can I go there and trust that a hand will be there with guidance and love?"

Yes my friends, just waiting for you to knock on the door – to go within.

Some of you will be able to walk straight in, as you may be able to meditate quite naturally. Others will have to work at it, but it is achievable for all of you, every single human being born and yet unborn. It is your gift.

Everything you see, feel, touch, and sense is what God is … there is nothing that God is not.

Crossroads

Your stance in life has brought about many questions, and trying to find the right answer, can sometimes feel like looking for a particular grain of sand in the desert. In the final analysis, you may come down to some questions about yourself that enable you to cross a particular bridge, and the answers you get back sometimes only reinforce your views on the frailty and emptiness of man. Therefore, perhaps you can see how one person's view may alter throughout their life because of their personal life experiences.

Of course, this is a natural process, but to have one's beliefs, and dare I use the word faith, shaken and embattled so frequently and violently, leaves you to question whether you are on the right track at all. It leaves you wondering whether you have a handle on the scheme of things or not? If you have maneuvered yourself into a place of harmony where you may spring from – where you may gain further understanding.

Still, it is up to you, as it remains to be seen whom you would wish to align yourselves with. Perhaps no one, for each of you journey as a star upon itself, as an individual. It is only mankind who wishes to be as part of a herd.

The closeness and the bonding within your unit and sphere of life, means you can all be like sounding boards for ideas, explanations and intelligence, which enables you to understand and grow with one another. Otherwise, you could seek a lonely reclusive existence, becoming like the hermit and shunning all who may pass.

On the other hand, you may seek only your higher self. Which is a good place to be, and I do not doubt that effort, but for you in your journey, you need to react and inter-react with people, because the need is so great there.

Both you, and those with whom you mix, must learn further knowledge and have greater awareness pertinent to your unfoldment. Such knowledge and awareness is there to increase your understanding about love, harmony, fear, and doubt. If you have gained these lessons then eventually you may be able to steer others into directions that will be right for them and provide them with greater balance.

In reality, you have to allow people to experience for themselves who they are, all of their faults and everything, but just be there. If they truly wish to progress, they will put those faults to one side, and simply not accept them as part of their life. They cling onto their faults like garments, as if they are cold.

You have to teach them that actually, you do not need to wear that many garments in the summer of your life, and how light it feels without them. Show them that when you walk with spirit in your heart, when you are in touch with yourself, you do not have to pick fault with people, or criticize and throw negative feelings and thoughts in the directions of those who do not walk your walk.

You will arrive at many crossroads, and many times, you will say: "What is the point in this, why am I here at this place again – how can people do this?"

My friends, you have so much learning to do, and it is so difficult to fit it all in one lifetime, all in one go. A practice you may seek is sometimes obscured by clouds, by the forests of negativity and doubt, by a mountainous region that seems impassable. Yes, you should look to the sides, and occasionally behind you to see where you have been, to make sure you are not going round in circles. But I assure you, you are not – it is just that sometimes, levels of understanding takes a few goes to get right.

People are really a composite. They are made up of other people's views and ideas, and so because they have taken on board thoughts and feelings from other people's experiences, sometimes all of those little parts together, do not actually make them the individual they truly are. Try to remember, that certain people may not know what they are doing either. They can be confused and can make drastic mistakes, because of all the things they have to deal with in their lives.

You may think: "Oh my, what on earth can I do here? I cannot help this person, because they are being so stupid, so unwise. Yet, I thought that they were intelligent – they were held so high in my estimation. I thought they were where I wanted to be, that they had some hidden treasure I wanted to bring out in myself."

However, my dears, you cannot bring it out in yourself because it is not your treasure. What you have to find is your treasure, your little spark of life. Your little energy ball that needs to be developed within yourself so that you yourself will learn who you are. Everyone has their own method of getting there, but what you need to learn is what makes you tick. How you progress upon your journey is up to you and not anyone else.

So as a result, if a person whom you may love and admire, completely misses the point as you see it, it is just a fragment of their life journey they have had to learn by. It is their life – you cannot live it for them, so you just have to let them get on with it and hope they will know what they are doing. If they do not know what they are doing ... well, they might be of a mind that you cannot tell them anyway, so you can only be truthful and honest with yourself and your own feelings and walk your own walk.

Then how can we help or influence? How may we spread any of these words or any of these thoughts and feelings, if we are locked in our individual little bubbles, struggling with ourselves, wrestling with our nerves and minds, trying to beat them into submission to get them under control? How may we do this and deal with the great outside world? How may we also deal with our spirit pathway and teach others?

The answer my friend, is that you cannot. Unless you can teach yourself. Unless you can become in harmony with yourself. Unless you can tread most respectfully and lightly upon the planet surface, listening, watching, and taking it all in, you cannot hope to begin to learn how to love.

If it should be, that you come upon those folk who ask of your knowledge, then that is the right time – that is the right time to communicate.

Now, this does not mean to say that you just sit and wait in your shoebox for someone to come along, but what I mean, is that those who are seeking will happen by you.

Seek the higher mind, seek that greater love friends, those loving arms of spirit are holding you now. Feel joy and peace in your surroundings and within your mind. Keep all your thoughts in the best possible manner. Not muddy or clouded, but clear and wise, and when asked, always give your best council ... to move both them and you forward into the light.

Truth does not lie or nest
With thoughts of evil deed
For that vibration
Has no life of its own
And must cling to the truth
That has an abundance

Certainty

It is with much love that we come and hopefully, bring brightness, love, and certainty where there is none. The certainty about which I speak is that of your progression through life and the certainty that you will not die however hard you try. Your physical body becomes no more, but the essential you remains, and it is dependent upon the climate of the mind as to how much of this life is retained, how much of it you will take with you.

However, you may wonder how you can remember who you are if you do not have a physical body to recall it for you. If you no longer have a brain to signal various chemical and biological actions upon the mind, to release certain bits of information.

Well, your mind has nothing to do with your brain, as your mind is a separate entity. Your mind is a layer of the spirit form, a layer that is similar to the auric form. It is this, which is linked with the spirit by the vehicle of the soul and all of this survives physical death.

The duty of your physical body now, is to put you in touch with all of these aspects of yourself if it can, if there is not too much opposition. Of course, this can depend on how you have been brought up. How you have evolved and if you have recognized your certain inner qualities or not. All will depend upon whether this journey has been successful. Quite simple really, there is nothing complicated about it; this is it in its entirety.

Having said all of this, do not think that your journey must be insignificant in relation to such an awesome subject. Far from it. Each one of you is on a completely significant journey to the whole. Each one of you an intimate aspect cherished. The relationship between you and other fellow humans, fellow creatures, all who walk beside each other, are all completely linked.

Therefore, you cannot feel you are not worthy or that you are too good. It is better to see yourself as just who you are and try to improve on it in your own small way, than to dress yourself up into something you are not. The thing to do my friends is to wash your ego away. Throw it out with the rubbish and let the dustman collect it in the morning.

If you wish, you may acquire everything your journey needs, and we, in spirit, will do everything we can to help. We will be as active as possible in your support, and in doing so, we may also gain understanding into things that we too have not yet learnt. We too, may grow and help you to grow, for it is a part of our life journey, and most spirit will be of service at some time or another as part of a general evolution.

Each one of you has a simple journey. Make the most of it. Every moment that you have is yours to experience for your benefit. I know this may be very hard to take in sometimes, and you cannot always help the things, which happen in physical life, whether you bring them about or not. Do not worry, for you are all safe in the arms of the eternal spirit.

Armies can be used
To fight with swords of truth
But truth says
I want no part of armies

Parallels

When you walk down the street how much notice do you take of those people who walk in the opposite direction? You may make mental observations about how a person looks: whether they are beautiful or ugly, large or short, for you have such a diverse picture of each other. All of these people who cross your vision are a part of the eternal life force, and each has an individual spirit locked up within, traveling with them upon their journey.

All of those different little aspects are like a mirror image of God, for that is what they are. You cannot say that one person is any closer to the divine entity than any other, for all human beings who walk the path upon the physical plane are all walking a similar path. Although, each path may be vastly different in your concept of what is similar.

You could have two situations that run in parallel. They may be completely different situations, but very close. Yet, if you used a wide spectrometer with which to look at these two objects, you would be able to show that the distance between them was as great as could be, as vast as you are standing to a building half a mile away.

You see, it is only how you perceive it, for half a mile away, could be almost touching within the actual scheme and make up of the eternal spirit. Therefore, you are not as close or as far away as you think, it is only a matter of your perception of the situation. You may find many aspects and avenues defy all logic, for it is only your mind, which can accept or not, the various principles spread before you.

I know it may be difficult for you to conceive of an idea of a world that runs in parallel and within and without your own. Most people on your side would probably think this is just preposterous imagination. It is not any kind of psychological problem that you have, it is not that you are becoming unbalanced my friends. Rather, it is about you perceiving the truth, the truth about you, and the nature of your world around you. In knowing this, you might then cease to make the mistakes you do and proffer a different direction. You may offer yourself to a different climate of reasoning in whatever manner. It has got to be better than what you are doing right now, and this is not you wishing for an idealistic solution to your eternal problem of death.

The fact is that you are progressing in some ways within your sciences, for the benefit of those around you, but you appear to be working in the opposite direction in others. You are yet unable to comprehend the fact that there could be (and are) other dimensions that exist, which you cannot and do not relate to.

If you become awakened and aware of the spirit within you, then at least you have a chance to perceive new ideas.

Power and Control

There are very many on the physical plane who are perhaps feeling stronger than they are. Feeling as if they can conquer everything and use their physical strength to out-maneuver their fellows. They see it as a vehicle for getting what is wished for. Of course, there are those who just like to feel physically fit, but there are also those who enjoy its power and have a wish to be dominant. And that physical power, I wonder if it matches your egos?

You might have to be careful as to what kind of a balance you struggle to achieve. What nature of harmonic distortions you commit within your mind frame to bring about the perfection you seek in your physical body. It is very commendable that one may seek to establish such rigorous attitudes towards physical capabilities. However, you also need to practice with your mind. Engaging it to a mental agility that takes you to the place not so far removed from where you will find spirit. Indeed, you are then tuning yourselves to the spirit within you, in achieving the will to dominate your physical body.

I am not saying any of it is right or wrong, it is your journey, it is your wish to excel, and so you should. It is good to push borders, for humanity to extend themselves beyond the boundaries previously laid, because it gives a sense of fulfillment and joy.

You can have different situations, whereby people use their physical strength to dominate and oppress; it has been the age-old pestilence of the world in which you live. From generation to generation, there have been those who dominate, and I suppose, they look to nature to reassure themselves that what they do is right. The weaker of the animals become the hunted and are slaughtered in the name of the progress which is felt is made ... 'they have survived and surpassed all those who lay beneath them!'

Except, everyone will grow weak eventually, in the physical sense, and physical strengths are not everything. Boundaries and limits are only what humanity has set and there are goals you may reach and surpass, and all of these in time will be broken. Such is man's will that there will become a time when they will decide they cannot go any faster or further. That they cannot run any faster or swim any faster because it is just not physically possible, as the bones and structure will not allow it and the density of the atmosphere will not allow it.

Human beings have pitted themselves against each other for centuries upon centuries. Yes, it is very good to be fit; if you have a fit body, you may have a fit mind. If you are lazy, you could become encumbered with your laziness and sloth, and then become what you might call a 'couch potato.' It is in every walk that you walk, and one is no different to another, they are all excesses. Whether or not they are excesses that you choose, of course, is a matter for you, as is your sexuality. Anything to do with the way in which you live your life is a matter for you and your preferences, for you are living it. You must fulfill your dreams and desires.

There is physical dominance over someone else and there is physical aggression, which is entirely different, for some of you might wish to become physically proud in order to be aggressive. Again, this is another story, and one should you wish to follow, will lead to its own conclusion. Mankind can be so complicated, but you can also be so simple. You all have different ways, all of them different aspects of trying desperately hard to be individual, but at the same time following someone else's idea.

I know this does not happen all of the time, but for many, the thought when you are in school is, what can I do to make my living? What can I do with my life? And very often, what you automatically think of is what other people are doing. Then rather than seeing your own full potential, as to who and what you are, you embark upon another course of someone else's – of who and what they are or were – of what they do or did.

Of course, there is no problem with that, you have to live your material life and it is up to you to try to make the best of it. Yes, you have to make a living if possible, but I would have to say that in you choosing somebody else's thought or activity, although you may enjoy your work, do you perhaps sometimes feel there is something you have left out? That there is something you have missed within your relationship with yourself. It is no good saying who you are if you do not know.

If there are certain aspects of yourself that you find a little disagreeable, and yet you feel it is too late to change, well, it is not. With all these things, it is never too late to put things right. It is never too late to make amends for a past wrong.

It is not to say you should seek complete absolution of all blame or wickedness, like going to the confessional box; but even if you get to the age of eighty-six and you discover there is something else within you, it is not too late my friend. At least you have discovered it, so it is not a wasted journey is it. You have had a good and happy life hopefully, and you have done what you wanted to do with it, and if you did not, well it is only because you took the wrong route. It is possible for everyone on the earth plane to come alive through the release of fear.

When you are building yourself up to be a big strong person, to dominate, just remember that when you come to our side it will all disappear. No matter how much you train. No matter how much you may exert yourself, you will become just like any other again, as you were before you began your earth journey. No matter what you do on the physical plane, it will eventually be that you cannot continue through physical inability, because things have stopped working. However, the spirit that you are will always be there – right up to the point and beyond your physical death.

Whatever it is you wish to progress and take part in, meet with fullness, meet with a knowing. Not of whom you can beat or whom you can be better than, but rather, who you are, and just that. Not the great 'I am,' but just try to be at one with and at peace with yourself. For you do not need to be physically big to be recognized in your true light, nor do you need to be as small as possible to blend and melt into the crowd.

You all need to stand out for yourself, not for selfish reasons, but for the greater good of everyone. Not only everyone that you meet now, but those you may meet in the future. The world you live on is a big place, and you will meet many fellow travelers during your time spent here. Treat them all with respect and love and you cannot go far wrong, and it will sit with you kindly.

It is better to seek the smallest knowledge
For the merest crumb of understanding
Can brighten the saddest day
Knowing what you will now
Gives your life a better chance
For knowing more tomorrow
So look with open eyes, heart, and mind

Life's Decisions

At times of trials and decision, you find you still have to check your judgment, because it is not quite in tune with that which you are. You turn it over repeatedly in your mind, seeing which hat fits and whether you should wear gloves or not, along with all those postures and gestures of wondering whether your anguish has a rightful place.

"Did I do the right thing?" "Oh I don't know, we'll wait and see."

Such important decisions to be made about your life can easily be met by taking the first thought that comes into your head, but if it does not feel right, do not do it. I know it is easier said than done, and it is fine for us, for we do not have the same physical restraints as you have. Only, the principal is the same, whether you exist on your physical plane or whether you are of the free spirit in the vast oceans that are the spirit world.

There are, of course, many decisions that you make about various aspects of day-to-day life, which will bear very little relevance to the final outcome between your life on the physical plane and the transition you make to our side of life. Then there are certain other decisions that may change the course of your life forever, ones that may bring you closer to your spirit. They may also bring you closer to the spirit friends, helpers and guardians, who are forever by your side and ready to enrich your life; who give you courage to move forward.

These important decisions are judgments of truth, and as these truth symbols come upon you, you will know deep within what they are, for they just shine out all on their own. They have their own luminescence. They have their own vibration that plucks the strings of your inner knowing. Even if you did not know that your inner knowing existed, it would still place right with you, with your very being.

The charm and magnitude of your aura achieves this for you, it amplifies every decision you make. The aura is the energy field that surrounds you, which carries the present enhancements of your life, and to this end, what you go through emotionally, physically and spiritually, is painted and formed upon it.

As life events transpire they leave their imprints, and when all movements of thought and action are done in love, made in honesty and truth, then your auric field gets brighter and has more content. It carries your jewels of destiny, if you like. It is like wearing a blanket with very intricate designs upon it, and it will become brighter and clearer with time. Your light shines brighter and so will you. Deep within, you will glow brighter and you will be happy having come to the right choice.

You see, real truths do not need decisions to be made by you, for they judge themselves; for they would not be there if they were not real truths. In addition, judgments that you make upon other people in your walk of life, well, they may just be decisions as to whether or not you involve yourself with those people, for in truth, you cannot make a judgment upon another. All you can do is to either accept or place yourself elsewhere, out of reach of the one you feel does not bind well with your spirit.

Of course, you may come across many upon your physical pathway who do not sing your song or walk your walk. It does not mean to say they are bad. It does not mean to say that you are bad for feeling as you do. It is just merely that you are not of the same vibration. That is all, and there is nothing more to be said. You may find the disagreement you have leaves and does not hold weight upon you. You can then carry on with a full and open mind, ready for the next encounter along the way.

You could say that much of it is out of your hands. As those in the physical world who are higher up in the pecking order from yourself, have an even greater power over your existence. Within a certain frame of action and inaction, you can deviate much from a course you had perhaps begun in your way of life. You could be traveling along a certain path and a decision taken elsewhere leads you to somewhere completely different. It is very difficult to place your trust, to put all that you are, in the hands of another.

Almost impossible you may say, because like you, they are spirits having a human experience. How far can you really trust them or their words? They all have their own agenda, their own goals to reach, and you do not fully know how they would operate in your defense, on your behalf. Neither, whether they will take your feelings into account. It is very difficult to argue as to how you might place trusts such as these within the arms of others, for truly, really, you cannot. You can only trust yourself and then sometimes even that becomes very difficult in certain situations.

However, with all those decisions you have to make, make them for your benefit and not through anger. I know there are some strange people who would certainly make you angry; who have odd ideas about their place and rights to do as they wish. People who commit serious crimes etc or just people who rub you up the wrong way. Just leave them to themselves; leave it, do not let their negativity or their destructive forces enter into your auric field.

I am not saying that you just walk around with your eyes shut. You should digest all of the information that is necessary, and process it to conclude whether you feel a particular subject is right for you, or a certain taste, smell or vibration of person. It is all the same thing, just different facets. There are so many intricate details to your path. The trick is not to be waylaid and burdened by negativity and all of the other things that are so prevalent upon the physical form and the physical life you lead. You may steer your pathway clearly between the obstacles confronting you and there will be lights to guide you. There are us, in the spirit world, we are here to help. All you have to do is ask.

Remember this the next time you are faced with a situation that you cannot for the life of you fathom your way through. There are many roads to freedom. All of them are clearly marked and all are sign posted – it is just a matter of you reading the map to work out your journey.

If you have negativity
You may wash it from you
With the clear water of love

If you have hate
You are ill and need care
To welcome you home

If you have pain
From any of those
Who see you wrong
Look to your own inner well
To draw the love you will need
To better your spirit
And care for your feelings

May they always
Be bathed and healed
By the sensitive light of God

Exploitation

In that great light journey of your mind, in that physical struggle through the universe, there are some things, which are necessary for you to travel through in order for you to reach a certain place in your life. The struggle of whether you will 'make it' or not, whatever 'it' is. And when do you consider that you have? Is it when your bank balance shows enough zeros?

For many, poverty is the only zero they will ever see. They cannot ever seem to rise above it for their whole country maybe structured that they should remain there, and this is very puzzling. Mankind seems to be able to sit back and actually exploit the poverty that surrounds them. Perhaps not knowingly, but unknowingly it can be done, with sleight of hand from the ones who do the exploiting so that you do not notice. "Oh well, its better than they had before!"

The markets and the way the economy moves across your world, leaves in its wake a set of people marooned, as if after a violent storm. Because no sooner does their standard of living rise, and the feeling of need for further increments upon their wealth, that the trade moves on and they are left high and dry.

There can only be true balance and real understanding once the richer nations of your world become less dominant and dependant in some respects, upon the poorer ones. How else can they make vast amounts of wealth, if they do not employ cheap child labor or exploit the physical dimensions of the country involved? Exhaustively, they take all of the minerals away until there is nothing left, leaving only poison and waste, then withdraw and go on searching for more elsewhere, in an insatiable manner.

I suppose you could say this is operating with a free will, but it is also carelessness, just to realize easy money, without thought or planning for the good of the indigenous peoples. It still persists and it will go on. It will sweep through country after country that is in poverty or in dept to the richer nations, and the misery will be exploited. They may be from another country as immigrant peoples or from another area, or perhaps the north verses the south. It is all exploitation my friends, no matter where you are from.

You can even have exploitation of the mind. Some are clever enough to manipulate themselves into a position of power in order to control others. It is exactly the same thing; it is using and taking without consent, without their knowing the full picture, for people are only too pleased to serve. Are only just too pleased to take home the little bit of reward they may get, whether in terms of money, food, or favor. Whether it is physical or soul food, it is all the same, it is all exploitation.

You could say the same thing about the ministries that ran into Africa and South America, squashing out the old religions so they would have more power themselves. Anyone who was not of that ilk or understanding was an outcast. Well, it is still going on my friends; it is still the same and not just the province of past times. And when do you think you might decide to change it, for you are fast running out of planet?

Exploitation

We do not say that you must accept spirit, but please accept that we exist. It is entirely up to you to make the understanding – your choice. It is necessary that you must be guided, for you do not seem to realize in your searching for cheaper and cheaper produce, just how devastating an imbalance can affect the lives of people, and the misery that is created.

We recognize there is obviously a need for change, for reconciliation. The order as it is must be dispelled for there to be new beginnings, for new horizons to be realized. Forget debt. Forget old custom. Old custom can become worn out and irrelevant.

If you wish to go on buying and doing what you are doing, then increasingly you will blindly accept it and not have the will to stop it. Putting less and less value upon the life that you have … for you put less and less value on the life of those you exploit.

Letting Go

As you journey through your life, you tend to collect all sorts of material possessions until you end up with a whole attic full that you do not know what to do with. I expect most of you still have items you never thought you had.

It is the same with life baggage. You carry it along with you. Many of you try to hide it. You put it safely away in a box, and occasionally dust it off and look at the various memories and thoughts you have acquired through your life. Many of them are probably considered nuisances or annoyances to the mind that you would rather best forget.

You may find that with some of them you cannot. Some of them will stay with you for a very long time, and others, well they are just the waste. Much of it you can just throw away, for you have not thought of it for such a long time, so why let it bother you now?

You see, life is only really like that if you let it be. Yes, agreed, many things upon your life journey that you take on board are necessary, but they become lessons that you must learn by. Once you have learned them you move on.

Does it make you any better a person for carrying them with you? How big a trailer will you need? How big a cupboard in your life will you need? All of the trappings in your life and how you were towards people; all of those memories and the sheer embarrassment at the recollection of them.

You know: "Oh gosh, did I really do that then?"

Well yes, I mean you were growing up and you maybe did not know any different, so it is not such a big deal is it. You can simply forget them friends, as you have moved on so far since then.

There are consequences of actions you have taken, which you might feel have irreparably damaged your life, but they too, were just lessons that you had to learn and the things you had to go through. It may well be that the other fellow spirit travelers that you have met on your journey, had to go through those situations too.

There is the whole interactive situation with your physical life. You meet so many people, and all of them interact with you and play with you. They do their own learning with you. Some on your account and those painful little pieces can also be put to one side, but not necessarily discarded, for they may be of use later as a recollection to save you from making the same mistake again.

Hopefully, you will learn these lessons that are set for you and those who you come into contact with; that they too will learn their lessons, all interchanged between each other, so you can grow. Much of this is attached to affairs of the heart, of the loves won and lost, of the instances of near fame and fortune and of near desolation and remorse. All mixed energies and all there to bring you to the one spot eventually upon your life journey.

My friends, you can put all of these recollections of unhappy memories in such an inaccessible place, as you will not be able to find them in days or years time. You do not need to resurrect those painful parts of your journey; you do not need to bathe in their reflection. They are all honest mistakes, which you do not have to carry around any longer. You can just set them down and I am sure you will feel very much happier for their weight no longer being upon you. Then you can breathe safely, without taking in the dust, and your mind can be free to do the work that you need to do to move forward. The work with who you are now, at this moment in space.

You see, for although you are living on a planet, you are still in space my friend, for only in your dimension are you sitting. For all you know, in all other dimensions you could be upside down, lying horizontally and facing in a completely different direction, or standing on your head!

It is only your perception and understanding, and as soon as your understanding expands, the less frightening your predicament becomes. You will become gladdened by the realization that all is not what you thought. That although rarely seen in your dimension, truly in ours, it is full of life and everything you would wish for it to be.

Be not afraid be not tearful of your plight
So much awaits you within the truth of realization
You too are glorious
An amazing testament to the love sheltered within you
You may all gain strength and courage
To make your place within the framework of life
There is not one person who is unworthy
Not one soul who may not enter in
None are singled out for punishment
As you will all be your own judge throughout eternity
In life eventually all are equal.

Where There is a Will

Everyone makes a journey along the corridors of life on your planet and in one way or another, the manner of communication you use sounds and rebounds, disturbing the peace fields. Imagine living in a small flat in the middle of a city and everywhere around is music, laughter, crying, speaking, shouting, snoring – a cacophony of sound. All of that humanity going on around you like it is coming out of the walls itself and you cannot shut it out. Some people do have to live like that; they are forced to live in very, very difficult circumstances. I think you could say that it is no wonder many people turn to drink and drugs, because it is just a product of your way of life.

As a result, how in amongst all of that noise can you find any peace or stillness?

Well, even there my friends, it is possible for you to find peace without interference. Somewhere in the middle of the little island that is you, there is a cave where you may dwell, a cave that is warm and loving where you may feel protected and safe from the world outside. A place within – where you can be with your spirit.

You can still be in the midst of the noise, but you can shut it out, because in your meditation you can get into a certain state where it just fades into the background, and becomes like any other noise or any other silence. Noise and silence are only your perception of them. They only disturb you if you let them disturb you. This is something you can do that will effect how in control you feel; where with practice you could have more ability to stop such interference from coming into your mind and so bring it under your physical control.

Some people from your side of life do not enjoy the silence, and like to have and to make large amounts of noise all of the time, but it is all entirely dependant upon your walk and how you wish to tread. You can make something out of everything that surrounds you. Everything to do with your life you can use to good effect. It is just a matter of taking the initiative to do so.

Friends, if you wish to get in touch with yourself you do not have to be on a desert island to do it. You have your own island within you and you can go there whenever you wish. You do not even have to step out into the street. You do not have to pay for it, except perhaps with some of your time, and that is something you must come to terms with and set aside for yourself. It is your time – where you may just be.

You live on a planet, a physical existence and yes, I agree, in your learning processes you also have to understand all about how you may survive on it, but that does not take every day of your life. You begin that journey yourself in earnest at a very early and tender age. In fact, as soon as you become aware of your physical form.

Investigate and initiate some new questions upon your mind, upon your thoughts, not the tired old dogmatic ones. They are worn out their pages are all curled. The words fall off the paper and they put up walls and barriers for you to find success within yourself. For what they do is lead you to give the responsibility to someone else, so that everything you do is either through God's punishment or through God's love.

Well, I am sorry friends, there is no punishment other than by thine own hand, and thine own thought – for thy wickedness thine own poison. Take as many opportunities as you can. You can alter what you do not like about yourself so there is no excuse really; you just have to have the will.

Your house is everywhere. You do not need a large building to go to. You are your own house and you can go to your own inner temple whenever you wish. There is no admission fee and you do not have to pay the price with your soul in purgatory or damnation if you do not go. The only price you will pay for not going within is to remain ignorant of the truth. If truth is what you seek, it is all in there – you only have to look.

Conflict of Thought and Racism

There can be so much conflict within your life, even when you do not realize it. You could be just sitting there eating a piece of toast and your mind can be in a turmoil, worrying about what is happening or what might or might not happen. Certain ramifications that can affect you, may lead you to wonder whether it might be the beginning of a downward spiral for you. Will there be another uphill struggle in order that you too may find happiness? There are so many battles and so many roundabouts, that if you are caught in them you could get thrown around for years.

You require real thought, real imagination upon the truth. You need imagination sometimes, to skirt around what has obviously been put into your head; ideas that were placed into your mind by the negative forces and vibrations that are around you. Sadly, in accepting this into your life you became a part of that negative vibration, so you must lift yourself out of it. You must try to progress upon your journey with a new and enlightened mind, open to reality.

The fact is, even without thinking, people generally tend to sift out what they do not automatically agree with or have an affinity with, without perhaps giving any further thought to the subject. There is so much information, which is relevant to you or may well become relevant to you, and the obvious bigotry and disharmony you may encounter, they are the signals for you to make a right or left turn. Not to block them off altogether you understand, because you must learn their full content, to recognize bigotry and racism within you and within others.

For instance, if you do not like a Chinese person, a black, or a white person, discover why not.

Ask yourself: "Is that view wise? Is that view the truth? How has it come about? Is it someone else's view?"

It may be something that actually happened to you or it may be a build up over many years of stories or films. Of how you perceived a character, or how a race has been portrayed.

If you go into a Chinese restaurant, does the waiter then suddenly attack you, or act in whatever way you had previously imagined? No, of course not, but all of these things influence your idea, maybe even before you had met one in real life. You may live in a town or country that has very few people of other races in amongst them, and in that case, there may be much hostility when they arrive. Such views are unfounded.

You cannot judge others and you must be careful. If you allow the conflicts to go on, to rage across the plains of your mind unchecked, they will battle on relentlessly my friends. Conflict of thought makes you sick, tired, and worn out. You need to be able to understand rather than let ideas dictate and war among each other. You need to look at both sides of the coin in order to resolve dispute. It is the same with any ideology. Like any fact or fiction that is presented to you on your journey. You must look at both sides, and decide for yourself what you would wish to do or use as part of your physical philosophical mental make-up.

Your progress is not only about how we, in spirit, may interact with you, but about how each of you may interact with each other, and these are some of the things you all seem to find so difficult. It really does worry us and perplex us at times, as to how people can be so negative towards those of your races who are different to yourselves. It worries us that racial inequality exists, as it has for many eons of your time, for there have always been slaves and masters.

At times, possibilities arise where you could break those taboos and boundaries, where you may actually learn to live together in harmony, if the various people concerned would only allow it. There are many instances when people of all different nationalities can gather and give without thought of themselves, without thought of what they have, but just give to those who have not. You know it really does gladden us that man here upon the physical world is actually capable of doing this regardless of all the negativity that surrounds him. We are very happy that en masse you are still able to make good deeds, so it does prove that it is possible. It proves there does not have to be this bigotry, this racial disharmony, this harping back to times in the past and living them repeatedly, for the sake of self-assurance, for the sake of their standing within their community.

There are those countries struggling for democracy, who then throw it away. They have the chance, but they reject it, or rather it is rejected by a few who are far more powerful than the poor peasant in the field. They are then driven along, unable or incapable of doing anything about the matters that drastically affect their lives, and are just consequences suffered via the few.

We, who have witnessed so many disasters, who have seen so much deprivation on behalf of humanity, we deal with it continuously. Therefore, it gladdens us when there are prospects of furthering human accomplishment and emotion, of giving love freely, of being able to help another soul in distress. Not necessarily one nation to another with the giving of food or clothing in times of disaster, but just as a matter of helping one another, of guiding across the stream of life – from one shore to another.

You must always remember as you do this, that that person may be blind even though they do not carry a stick. They may well not see what you see. They may not hear what you hear and their light may not shine as yours shines. However, you are the brightness by which they have been attracted, and they will be gladdened by your humanity and your gifts. Your many gifts of giving.

>It is the greatest treasure
>That we bring our lives
>To bear fruit to each other
>So we may openly see
>What gifts we bring
>We may come upon
>The flowers of truth
>Scent their air
>And cheer at their glory
>Elements of the greatest Lord
>Force of the universe
>The ultimate bead of love

Lies

Over many of your years, I have watched and seen how man has failed to improve. Has grasped to find a way out of his own responsibility to himself and to the planet on which he lives. I have never understood it.

Is it so much easier to lie? For when you lie, it sends a whole shock wave throughout the universe, for you have told an untruth, a situation that does not exist. You have altered and changed the course of your life forever, because everything proceeding that is also a lie. Then even if you try to get back onto the track of the truth, you find it very difficult.

For instance, if you wrote a book that is an untruth, but called it a truth, you are not only doing a disservice to truth, you are creating a disharmony within yourself and with those around you who may come upon it. Will you declare at the end of the book that it is a lie? No! You may say it is truth and deception arrives you see. It deceives the unknowing mind of the fellow spirit traveler.

Just think of the amount of devastation this creates, considering someone's whole life and path may have been shaped and determined around this deception. One lie can lead to many disasters and this is true of your history, for throughout history, mankind has lied to each other in the process of gain for themselves, gain for their country, and gain for power.

Truth in your world can play such an important part, but I fear now, that people on your side have not heard the truth for such a long time, they do not even recognize it. Even the highest of your people, your politicians, men of religion, whatever; they do not meet your expectations of what the truth is.

Their truth is not necessarily your truth. People have become so blasé about telling lies and hearing lies. They accept lies as part of their daily ritual of contact, bravado, of jousting with each other so that it becomes like a kind of a game, to see who can come nearest to the truth without actually saying it. However, the truth is very obvious when it is presented as such.

There is a saying that the truth hurts. It is so often painful perhaps, because generally, humanity is just used to living within a lie, within a fantasy world of thought and thinking. That all manner of places where mankind would wish to have as his preserve, is held within the hand of God, within the hand of a dominant yet bountiful sire; and mankind himself is whispering in the wings whilst waiting to go on to do his part in a play. As we observe from our viewpoint, it feels like for much of the time, man is in deception with his fellow man.

Of course, it goes much further, because it is not just neighbor and neighbor; it is company and company. People send pieces of hardware out into space and on purpose do not make it in the right manner so that a mistake is made, so the truth cannot be found out. What manner of planet, what manner of desire within the human mind frame would wish to perpetrate such dishonesty? Does mans wish to control

Lies

and dominate all those around him mean so much that he should send his fellow man into the long spiral of lies?

Until people on your side of life fully understand the ramifications upon which each untruth is told, they cannot hope to gain knowledge and wisdom. For everything else is false. You cannot realize your dreams and ambitions if you dwell in deceit. However, for a while deceit has a very good trick to play, for it can make you believe yourself and can make you walk down a very long and rocky pathway.

The first deceit you make is like opening a gate into the garden of bad fruit. You need to make sure each piece of fruit you pick is ripe. Not over ripe so that it tastes foul, and not under-ripe, for then it will be sharp and not to your liking.

Truth is a happy flower and always worth leaving as part of the plant upon which it grows. To be treated with respect. To be admired as it blossoms, with the brightness that exudes from its petals.

Do not Leave Negativity to Chance

If you catch sight of a speck of cloud upon the horizon in an otherwise clear sky, do you think it is going to rain? As you observe the speck moving closer, is it possible that it will alter your perspective? Is it also possible, that as it moves overhead, you see right into it … and then it passes you by?

Well, negativity is just the same. You can sometimes see it in the distance or feel it coming relentlessly. You do not want it, but it comes nonetheless and slowly it sweeps over you. Yet, all the while, if you stayed calm and just acknowledge its existence and read nothing into it, then it can get nothing from you and it may dissipate from your sight, from your thought and from your senses. It will seem like those negative energies were never really trying to get in, in the first place; that they formed like clouds, but just washed over you.

Indeed, it is just that you and it, happened to be in the same place at the same time. This is not very difficult considering there is so much negativity on your planet at the moment. It may pick upon anyone at anytime, but it is up to you as to whether you allow your spirit to become infected. You must treasure the spirit that you are. Look after it and grow it like a treasured plant in a greenhouse, which you would never leave out in the frost.

Do not leave things to chance. Always be diligent in your efforts to increase your awareness, to increase your efficiency with your senses finely tuned, but above all, to let love flow within and without you. Remember, love is so much stronger than negativity, and it may blow those negative impulses and circumstances away.

Friends, there are only a certain number of clouds in any one sky and the sun usually manages to push through at least once a day. If each person greeted the mornings with positive forward thinking, then the nature of your thoughts would be far more uplifting. They would spread with the dawn with an equal amount of light, welcomed with a positive outlook.

"Oh good, it's the morning, how beautiful – thank you."

Instead of: "Oh no, not another day!"

I am aware that much of this downhearted view first thing in the morning must be due, in part, to your physical and material existence. Still, when you live and work in negativity my friends, you need all the help you can get in order to cope with it, and it is really quite prevalent in the human condition. It causes much disease, much suffering, and a shortening of your physical life span, for every time you think of a negative thought or have a negative feeling towards someone else, you are also doing damage to you. You are lessening your own light.

Thus, think about how the light from each of you, combined with that of the sun, combined with that of the spirit light, could be such a positive and forward thinking force. You probably think I am dreaming, but it can happen. You are a physical being with a spirit that is having this experience, and it is most important that you recognize what you are capable of.

Do not Leave Negativity to Chance

You see, when you are within the spirit world, you do not have the chance to move forward in the way that you can when you are having a human experience. When you are in the physical, energies are presented to you in a way you do not experience when you are on the spirit side of life. We experience a myriad of other things – it is just different.

There are certain aspects of the human nature that are only learnt in human form and nowhere else, and that is why you are here. There are certain aspects of love that must be learnt through the negative forces that surround you, in order to establish a different pattern upon the way you live and react. This is no mean feat either for they are everywhere, but you must try to balance your mind and remain in equilibrium.

When you are opening up within, you will find that the morning will bring positive focus and fresh thoughts, with new feelings of wonderment of how much you have accomplished. That some of the previous hurdles of life, which seemed so big at the time and took such a lot of effort to overcome, were actually, huge strides upon your journey. And precious to the world of spirit also, for we will all of you to make steps, to make adjustments to your life and bring the realization that you are forever.

It is not cheating death. Death has a sad coat on this morning, because it realizes that it does not exist, and how much of a sparkle it puts into your life knowing that fact. As each moment lays out before you, each realization of your life journey ahead comes into focus and your world becomes so much more uplifted. Your life and every fiber of your being comes into this focus and moment, with the realization that your life is continuous.

If your horizon be not of silver, be not of precious colors you so admire, let your love light your path. It will steer you to the special places within, where you may dwell, a new experience, testing times gone.

Spirit Walks with Gregory

Always there are ones to guide in harmony and love. Take this strong love; expand your inner consciousness to accept it with grace, with pleasure and free will.

All future is an open book
For they are pages not yet written
Words are not final or set in stone
Until they are upon the page of life

Be aware of every thought
As it comes upon your mind
How it may dance and to whose tune

Does it reflect your inner most fear or love
Is it a reflection of who you are
Or is it a part of that which you despise

Make every thought count
For they are precious
Yet still take energy
To formulate and muster

Dreams Not Nightmares

All through your life you make many countless wishes. Maybe you no longer wish to be involved with the mode and method of learning you had before, because you feel you have changed, evolved, and taken a different path. The whole of life is a learning process from the moment you wake and are aware of the smallest thing.

You all have dreams, which you have brought with you, but if your dreams are sent away, they may become distant – like posting a letter believing you may never get a reply. Such is your choice you see, for if you think you will never get a reply, then you will not. It is not to say that you hold on to false dreams either. When you think you have a goal that is set upon your life journey and it has all of the goodness in it, it has all of the richness that it deserves.

It could be a dream of being in harmony and in flux with the universe, or of knowing who and what you are. That dream would be sufficient for anyone. If everyone could have that dream then it could be so simple. But you do not necessarily sit and wait for your dream to come true do you? You do not just wait for the return of the mail that you sent. You get on with your life.

Yes, sometimes the thought of the dream is put on the back burner or even forgotten altogether and that is understandable, for as time passes so do many opportunities. So much can happen in your life journey that you may not think your dream is possible any more.

On the other hand, perhaps you just had the wrong dream, the wrong ideal, or the wrong idyllic thought. For sometimes friends, you do not realize what your dream of life is until you have stumbled upon it, or it has stumbled upon you.

Until suddenly, there you are sitting in it. Thinking how happy you are, feeling recognition, empathy, choice, and harmony.

You see, we are not talking of the dreams that you have on a daily basis, or the wanderings of your mind as to where you would wish to be. Frivolous, yes, you could be frivolous, you are allowed; you are allowed to do anything you wish. Sometimes, it can seem incredibly unrealistic to think of a given pathway and actually make plans for the journey constructed to arrive at that place. It is incredulous the way in which some people design their lives. However, it is a part of your life plan to recognize which is dream and which is reality, against those dreams that are unattainable and not your pathway.

Many people associate dreams as being a fantasy. Dreams are not about fantasy – dreams are an alternate reality that is all. We are not talking of course about the type of dreams you may have whilst you sleep, but the dream state of reality that can be there for you as a method of how you work out how you may get from A to B. It is a faction of your mind frame that lets you be aware of who you are on the inside. That lets who you are on the outside, be aware of that one on the inside. To come together and acknowledge the existence within you – of who you are.

At times, you may feel you *are* dreaming, and think: "Oh no, I won't do that that is not reality, that's totally out of my grasp!"

Well, it may be your journey my friend, it may not be out of your grasp, because things may just slot into their places for you to walk across the bridges that will make the reality possible.

It is not about your determination, it is about your seeking, your questions. You have to ask the questions if you are going to get any answers. Everything comes down to those who listen to the answer. In acknowledging the voice within you, you acknowledge your own existence. Listen to your mind and realize it is not you going mad; it is not you in a daydream. It is you in connection with you.

Each dream has a light, each one has an energy, not consuming, but guiding and kind. Those are the ones you are to watch out for. Not some wild fantastic scene, but glimpses of your harbor on this your earth plane, this your physical existence, linked with the spirit that you are. Then all will be blessed, for it will help you to bring about your journey to the aspect of God within you. To find your peace. To be happy with who you are. To resolve your disputes and be rested.

Be Yourself

We may only think that we mimic each other in certain ways, in the way we do specific things, like smile, walk, talk, or dress. We often adopt each other's personal mannerisms, and sometimes it is amusing to do this once in a while. Except for in life we tend to do it also, for we do not necessarily see why we are here, so we look to each other for answers.

"Oh yes, he is a bright fellow, perhaps I will go and ask him."

However, the answer that you get back is his answer, it is not yours, but you have an answer nonetheless, so it is something to work from. It is a step to take in a given direction. It may not be your direction, but you may take it to see where it leads you, for you may not have any other information with which to glean any knowledge as to the direction you should be taking at present.

That is until you happen upon another fellow traveler who also has an opinion that you may adopt. You may then go that way. Then combined with the knowledge of your previous encounters, you will gradually make up your own diagnosis if you like, as to whether those, whom you have been in contact with, make any sense at all.

If there are enough of you who think in a certain way (a standardized religious base that you have on your side of life is a prime example) you could have many sheep in the flock, though not necessarily because you have delved into the mind of reason. Looked deep inside you – to see what the truth says from there. Instead of this, you look to others to supply that truth.

How do you know what is in a jar of jam? You look at the label. It may have many ingredients in it you do not like, or that disagree with you, so you must read the label first to find out whether those ingredients are okay. Do the religious doctrines on your side of life carry a health warning? No! For you think that everything that proposes to be from the lips of God is true. That it must be true, if the claim is there and written down in black and white.

For example, yes, Jesus was a fellow spirit traveler of exceptional light. He was a healer and mystic of superior vision. He was a man who tried to open minds and show how to love. Very similar to you and I, just one of a higher vibration to you and I – but the message that he brought was missed.

Similarly, there are many teachers who have been to your side of life, who have tried to show how humanity may love each other and to respect all that is around them. But the anxiety, pain and distrust that your journey has brought to you (because what was in the jar was not what was on the label) has made you wonder just who you can trust, who you can turn to now.

You can trust the voice within you. You are all a part of God, so how can you not trust that inner voice? You do not have to go to the supermarket to find the right jam, you may go out and pick the ingredients one at a time and make your own. It will be sweet enough and to your liking and taste.

As is your spirit within. Just to your liking. It has no rough edges. It is boundless, and there is not one door you cannot walk through if you wish to make that journey. The journey is yours. You do not have to get a train, and you

Be Yourself

will not miss your destination. You may go there under your own volition. Your own free will, will take you. For when you go within, your will is Gods will. No mistrust, no anxiety, it is free for you to have. You do not have to put a coin in the box or sell your house. You do not have to keep somebody else in order to receive it. It is yours by right of life and there is no waiver.

Everything you encounter along your way must be treated with the utmost respect. It is your fruit for the jam you make. With loving care, as you mix the ingredients you will find that your spirit will grow and blossom.

If you see pain and suffering, negativity is felt deep within you. You will want to reach out and hold, reach out with the spirit light and give of service, a hand to lift and to guide in gentle arms. You need each other to hold onto at times. Man's spirit needs spirit from all walks of life, so that you do not stumble in the dark, but you will not, for it is only your fear of darkness that makes you stumble.

Sometimes, we may all feel we are negative. That the jam is bitter or that we have ended up with a piece of plain bread. There are some people on your side of life who do not even have that much, who eat less than the birds. A sad reflection of man's action upon his world at the present moment.

All of humankind on your planet now, has a hand in it. For you do have the communication to know what is happening on the other side of your world. Some of you may have money, material gain, and wealth, and yet you are not willing to lift a finger in service to help. You are all responsible for each other; you all contain the same jam on the inside. You all have a similar recipe, slightly different yes, according to taste, but essentially the same. You are all spirit, all of the same nature, and it is your walk to develop your nature to the best of your ability. If you cannot and you sink into the depths of negativity, then that is your journey my friend, and it is best that you try to drag yourself back out, for you will have to one day. If you refuse, it is your pathway and your journey. There are no penalties except your progress.

All is there before you and you will have many hills and mountains to climb. Gain your inner peace and you may share what you have with everyone you meet. Do not be afraid. Do not say what you feel and what you are behind your hand. Speak out, for there are many who do not or will not. There are many who would wish to know the truth. Discover who you are and make more of your journey. It is a never-ending encyclopedia; the more you read, the more you find out, the more pages there are in the book.

Those who live in fear prosper only negativity
To shut the lid is but a simple act
That requires courage of greatness

We may all move to show and direct
How we may recover our lives
To the inner light of love

How we may move forward again
Not in faith or hope
But in love and truth and peace

Just Do Your Best

Upon the earth plane, as you grow you expect that one day will follow another in a certain given pattern that makes you feel comfortable. One that makes you feel warm, safe, and snug, so that you may leave one comfort blanket behind to take up another. At times, your ego is out at the front steering your way through it all. It may be a big, bold, and bright ego, or it may be rather timid and not much of a sight at all.

Now, we are not talking about confidence or about being self-assured, we are talking about ego, brash – the 'I am!' To some on your planet, the 'I am' is the greatest gift of all. It surmounts everything and you fight for it. You fight for the right to have the largest ego there is. It seems the ego is something that is worshipped and people pay a lot of money for it.

How strange, when in sure fact, you lurch from one decision to another, and at any given moment, the reins of your life may be taken from you and you can be thrown into total disarray, by one simple action of another. How fragile your life is or can be that you rest all of your laurels upon the will and whim of others.

You are born, you get married maybe, and then you die. All three bring great employment to your realm, but none offers any kind of a respite in your long and arduous journey, seemingly so anyway. You may go through life in one form of employment, and throughout your life you may do your utmost for your charities. You long to belong to something so you may join everything you can think of, covering all eventualities, just in case. You pursue one idea after another and this is good, as everyone has to find his or her own direction, but it is because you are searching my friend, because you have this emptiness inside.

Everyone on your side of life has to become involved with something that will fire their imagination, something to be interested in. You need to find your journey and make the most of it according to your physical and mental abilities. You need to make the journey, which is most appealing to you, and if it does not succeed, then try something else. You have not failed, but maybe only set yourself too high a goal.

Life is like that friends. There may be many paths that come upon your road and you will have to decide which ones to take. Some may work out fine. Some may be perfect for you and let you flower, whilst others, well, they could be anything. You are all on a voyage of discovery. A journey that is meant for you to learn various lessons. Some may be very hard to take, while others are beautiful journeys of light.

You see, after having spent twenty years working at one particular thing, you may feel that it no longer holds sway for you or it is just no longer required to satisfy you, and this can happen more than once in your life. Maybe it does not hold the attention it once did and that you have become bored with it or that it has become bored with you.

There can be many reasons why you have to change your whole way of life and thinking. Some are there to try to get you to search in the right places for those things you might be inspired to create. You do not have to be in the same job, the same work for fifty years, and there should be no regret if you are not, for long has the time passed when one person stays within the same situation.

Your problem on the earth plane now my friends, is one of fear and worry, because you may have climbed too many rickety bridges too quickly, and ended up in a less than tenuous position. Wobbling, trying to hang onto any small root you can see, so you can cling on to your bricks and mortar, and cling on to your way of life, for you have become set. Do you see how it can be that if you are too rigid you can break with just a small knock?

Where are we going with this? What I am saying, is do not fear about what your life journey may be. Your life journey will happen regardless and in spite of your efforts to get it into a corner to knock it into shape the way you would wish, so you may put off your eventual demise. It will not happen. It may be many years down the line that you will discover you were deceived, as new horizons come forward and brighten your days.

You can accumulate so much wealth on your side of life and it will be all to no avail. All it means perhaps is that you may have a jolly time. Go on nicer holidays. Go to tiny corners of your planet where not many others have been (although, there are not many of those left). You can swim at the bottom of the oceans and play with the fish. You can experience many of the wonders and encounter many riches, but this does not mean to say that you will experience fully, that you take it in and on board with you. It does not mean to say that because you have done it, you know everything, or are any better than anyone else is.

The planet on which you live is your garden, and it is why you have to keep it as it should be kept. Yes, you are the guardians of your world, except you do not need to go through your life wishing for something new, to take your senses that little bit higher. To get you high on something or some event, just so you can say that you have been there and experienced it.

Experiences of life all add up, yes they do, but do you take the trouble to explore what there is though? Not to just gloss over it, but really explore it – to feel and open your senses. Your senses are your communion with your spirit, as to how you feel and react to given situations and how you may learn and bring on the advancement of that knowledge. Your feelings are there for you to explore. You do not need such a rigid structure. You are here to make a journey of discovery. A journey of life, whereby you recognize that the eternal life energy is within you.

It does not matter if you feel you have not made the most of your experience, so long as you have put in all the effort you can muster and have done as well as you can. Just so long as you have taken the trouble and made the utmost effort to understand what has been put before you and what you have left behind. We do not ask you all to be supreme masters in your understanding, for it will not happen. However, you can to the best of your will, make the most of your inner strength, and the more you use it the more it will grow.

Many teachers as they pass you by in their life have taught you these truths before, and whether you take any notice to what their life has manifested for you, is whether you appreciated it or not. If you can take it in, then it has indeed been worthwhile, for learning from any other life is worthwhile. As long as they are lessons for the good, for the betterment of humankind and for the upliftment of the spirit.

You are your own road, your own seat of learning and your own trial and error. Do not be bitter, it is a sweet life. Release your pain and suffering, let it fall like leaves to the ground and walk on, walk on my friends.

Positive Harmonic Propulsion

Positive harmonic propulsion is what can wake you up in the morning and give you a good day. It can steer you through minor irritations and carry you forward with focus, settled, and secure in your happiness. Positive harmonic propulsion can give you what negativity cannot.

Now, we all know about negativity, and the ills and ailments it can bring, we have delved into that deeply, but how do you make yourself positive? How do you stand up and be counted, if you do not have the will? If you are so broken by negative forces that you feel you simply do not have the energy to do it.

You can try positive reinforcement. You have to start the moment you are awakened into the conscious state from your sleep or resting time, with words like:
"I will." "I can." "I am strong." "I am calm." "I am worthy and loved." "I will be and become more attuned – I have this right!"

Do you notice the difference? It is not about giving you success on a plate. It is not about achieving all of those yearnings that you have. It is about stretching forward the 'I will' into 'I can,' and 'I will do,' and really *being* that positive force that exists. Why not use it, for it takes fewer muscles to smile than to cry, and once you have savored the positive harmonic force and seen what it can bring you will find life is a lot easier.

This is all very well I hear you say, for those who may be affluent enough to pick and choose what they do, but what if you are in a dead end job with no prospects?

Everyone has to start somewhere my friend. If you do not have any prospects of being positive in what you do, if you just shift endlessly from day-to-day and the whole of your life becomes a grind leaving you a shell of your former self, then you may start by changing your outlook. You can change your pattern of life.

Instead of dragging yourself out of bed unwillingly towards your daily toils and tasks, tell yourself: "I will … I will *be* this!"

You can change your mind. It does not matter how far along the road you are my friend, there is still plenty of time. There are still plenty of gifts you may give and receive, in the way of knowledge and learning, upliftment and love. Even if you have not had a physical partner for all of your time on your side of life, you may still move forward in harmony and balance with yourself. That the 'I will' will achieve 'what I wish.' This is not through negativity or through the detriment of another fellow traveler, but with the positive wavelength that you create by the 'I will' in love.

You will find the harmonic waves that surround you will propel you. You will notice that once you have tasted positive force, it is possible. Not regurgitating or recreating the same method or the same things, but foreword motion. Pushing onward, taking with it a new you. What you will discover, is that there is someone else in there waiting to get out, and the 'I will,' will take over. You can apply this to almost anything that you do.

If you think you are going to make a mistake, then you will. If you think you are harassed, then you will be. If you think bad karma, then it will come to you. You are never too old to learn my friend, even though you may have said a hundred times that you are. You most certainly 'can' teach old dog's new tricks, it just takes a little more time to sink in!

In your drift through life, never think that you have succeeded in negotiating all of the hurdles and barriers that have been put in your path. There are always obstacles, but it is how you perceive them. It is how you move to either avoid them or overcome them, and it is this mode that we wish you to take – that you learn to overcome them.

Agreed, it is better to cross the road safely and there are certain rules, which avoid being run over, but you can be completely positive and walk on a zebra crossing. In that way you will increase your chance of not meeting with an accident.

The harmonic forces that you encounter as you ease your mind into thinking in new directions will propel you through the day. You will find you will get to the other end of it and be surprised at how much is possible to fit into one twenty-four hour slot. Everything you thought was make-believe will come to fruition, not fantasy, but daily life.

You can apply the same analogy if you are in pain, if you are suffering a long and debilitating illness. I know it can be extremely hard to be positive when you are feeling the lowest of the low and depressed. Without sail is what you are, a ship upon calm water – locked within the agony.

Very often (and this is not saying there is something wrong with your mind) you are still within the agonies of yesterday and not in the present time, and those negative forces, those moments you encountered at that time, have stayed with you. Which is why spirit healers can very often spend considerable time in reversing the negative forces you have been in contact with, and why you may feel a sudden release during the healing process.

This is what negativity can do to you my friend – it can drag you right to the bottom if you let it.

All of that can be reversed, and 'I will' can put a smile back on your face and give a lift to your heart and mind. No ill can come of it. It cannot give you a bad time and it cannot wish you worse for yourself, so you really have nothing to lose. You do not even have to swallow your pride, for 'I will' can be within you. It will propel you into a brand new existence for yourself, and also those around you who have maybe noticed, but had not said anything.

Well, those who have shared your grief and sadness, can now share your loss of negativity, positive and uplifting, to help you to be able to push out of the bubble in which you find yourself – to break free.

You do not need to be an anarchist, but if you do find your life is disagreeable then make the change. Be positive. Things may happen around you for a short time that will still be of the negative influence, but all you need to do is to find that spark and you can move to the 'I will' and have a nice day.

It is with
Positive thought and focus
That with gentleness
Your march will continue
To acknowledge
That which you truly are
And not who
You are constantly being told
You are not

Values and Your Planet

Of course, everything cannot be perfect can it? Or can it? Exactly how much would you learn, if your life were perfect already, if you were just gliding across fields gazing at flowers with everything in it smelling of roses? Very idyllic, but this is the stuff of daydreams and not of your real world. Unfortunately, your world at this time is a much harsher place. What mankind tends to do is to retreat into a dream-like state to get away from negativity so that it does not bombard them constantly, that they have some relief from it from time to time.

Negativity induces a harmonic distortion about you and this is why it can make you feel so ill. As we have mentioned before, there are instances whereby you come into contact with negativity directly from each other and so feel the effects of it. This happens because you are an organism reacting with many others, thus it is chemical, biological and spirit. You are taking on board many signals from the outside and responding to them. Likewise, so does the earth, as it too, is an organism moving under its own volition.

When you take a step, you have to bear in mind that you should keep focused, that you are listening out for the ripples of the effect of your action; testing to see if there is any negativity to come back. And this, in respect of your planet and what you do to your food source and to your life, is very cumbersome. It is not a sensible way to move forward 'for the benefit of others,' for unfortunately, there are very many repercussions still to come as a result of the events that you have set in motion.

Yet, you still do not realize what they are. In denial and with arrogance, you still blindly push forward hoping against hope that your moves will not prove to be fatal. It is a very weak way of moving civilization forward!

You live on a world where there are an increasing number of you and you have a certain amount of space you may use either to good effect, or to leave unchanged or to go to waste. There is so much damage that you do without realizing or without caring, for care seems to be low on the priorities of materialism. Thoughts are living things, just as bacteria, bees, and flies; it is how harmony works. If you do not have harmony walking hand in hand with love, then the balance of your world can be upset.

You have to begin to work for those who are to come after you and in a manner that creates a sustainable future for the children of the future. You must do this without any arrogance and without being so selfish in your approach – without it being about control. This goes right across and throughout your life and those who do not seek to control or fail to control become depressed, because those who are successful are those who are controlling others. They are controlling you, controlling your life. It is like being given pocket money when you are a child and then having it taken away again a few hours later.

You see, all we are trying to do is to stop man so he may think, respond, be more positive than self-willed; to stop feeling he has to have a certain power over all others. Your power is only limited to your world, because when you arrive here within the spirit world, you are the same as everyone. On your world, you are the same as everyone too, for it is not a true power that you hold, it is only like holding a bubble in your hand, and at any moment, it can be popped by your own actions.

Think on this. Think on your progress and on what you feel you would wish to have, what you would wish to feel and know. Do you cherish your life really? The values that were instilled in you when you were young were not necessarily the right ones. Look to see if they rise to meet the challenges of your time. Look to see if they keep you in the harmonic balance or whether they distort your whole persona, the whole picture of what you see around you and what you feel inside.

You may alter it ... those values have not been given to you for life. They are just merely a starting gate, and you do not have to cling on to them in order to keep yourself afloat!

Through physical differences
We must make moves
To bring harmony back
Into the frame of life
Lest we forget
How it feels to wear
Lest we stop
Seeking greater things
For our children
To share

Responsibilities

Mankind has a very long history, it is possible to trace your lives and your ancestors back many hundreds and even thousands of years. The problem with history is that it sometimes dismisses previous lessons learnt as a folly of the time. Mankind, in general, continues to make mistakes and creates follies for himself, and yet you have all of that history stretching behind you to reflect on and learn the consequences of.

History has shown you all that if you strip the trees from a hill or a mountain the soil will be washed away, and you only have to look at nature to see it happening. Yet, man continues in the same strident manner, as if there was nothing to care about or care for. "It's only a hill!" However, so much life depends upon that hill, and much stability in the valley below!

As the population of your planet is now beginning to discover, there is no mystery to what we are saying, as the truth is coming to light, day by day, and week by week. How silly – how fruitless of mankind's desire not to better himself it seems, but to make the situation worse. Yes, there have been great advances in modern science matters, and it is a wonderful thing that people can live to such a ripe old age. It is wonderful that you can have a longer time on your plane to explore the avenues of the mind that you did not know existed. The problem is that everybody thinks they have all been there before.

Man has failed to realize that not all is actually, as he thinks that it is all panning out quite differently, and he has not even discovered the other dimensions yet. At least at the present rate, it is unlikely that humanity will venture out of its small solar system in a physical sense, not at least for a very long time. Which is probably just as well for the rest of the galaxies and planets and everything else that is out there. Nevertheless, it seems such a pity that you are able to waste so much on such a project, when there is so much that can be done for the benefit of all.

There are so many systems that you could bring forward, which would enable your planet to reverse its present decline. There are cures for almost all of the ills that occur upon the physical side of life within the arms of the natural world, but you are lessening your chances of ever finding them. Sadly, you are about to crush their very existence, through such things as the extinction of the rainforest regions and the pollution of the seas.

There have also been many developments that have been kept quiet, which would reduce the population's sickness that exist now. Many inventions are bought up and put on the shelf, or put in the bin altogether. What a lot of wasted energy, man's integrity in tatters. To think that those who are in the position to accept such marvels of technology are actually only keeping a tight lid on their own frail situation. We, in spirit, have also had a hand in these ideas, for we have influenced those of you currently in an earth-traveling mode for a very long time, whether realized or not.

Now, I am not being negative, I am not saying this without love or respect or for man's own wishes, but just to say that it is time that people stood for people, in a caring, sharing way. To give a hand, to help people to rise above their station at the present time. There should be no need for the poverty that exists now. Make yourselves better, not better than someone else, just better. That is the trick. It is not a matter of looking up to or looking down at another, but of looking eye to eye.

Pain will always be with man for as long as the truth is kept cloaked within superstition and fear. Humanity's journey does not end here, but is continued throughout the universe, for eternity. I know that you are not likely to say that you do not want to live forever, but it is true to say, you would not desire to live forever where you are now, for indeed, you would become mentally deranged and you would suffer greatly.

This brings us to another point, of the prolonging of life, as it exists here within your sphere. It is very good to see that someone may live to a 'ripe old age' as you would say. It is wonderful to observe that man can extend life by his own hand, and to save much suffering and unwanted transitions for those on your side of life who are not yet ready. It is well that you make your journey of life longer, but what good is an empty journey?

It must be fulfilled. It must be full of knowledge, of learning, of wisdom, all encountered and grown within. Otherwise, at the grand age of one hundred and thirty or whatever, if you are a vegetable, then you are not really very much good to anyone – least of all to yourself.

Of course, it is good that it has improved since the earlier times, when people passed at a very young age. Yes, there are benefits to the improvements that you have made and long may it continue. However, the body, your vehicle, has only a limited span. It has only a finite time to exist. What you need to do is to be able to get down to the bare facts and truths of life quicker, so you can learn more, so you can all see the truth for what it is. How it is explained is another matter.

There is so much responsibility involved with having and teaching children. Do not forget, your children are the future generations, and it is up to each of you to teach your children right from wrong as best you can. Not just your right and wrong, but universal. There are a myriad of laws within each given country and ideals are reflected within them. Some of them you may well dispute, some of them you may still regard as savage or abhorrent, and chastise and rebuff those who do not think as you.

Children that grow within your midst have a chance to perfect themselves through nurturing, so that they may formulate their own ideas and truths. Do not frown upon them, but admire them as one who has found their own way. I know that you have a dangerous field of possibility, but to insist that your offspring think and do as you do, is being nothing, but stagnant. It is being nothing other than holding that spirit and their free will to an entity of the past.

Do you want them to grow up just like you? Do you wish to perpetuate the stance that you take? Or do you wish for them to grow with fresh ideas? As shiny new spirits having a human experience for themselves … under their own volition, and within their own right.

Indeed, they learn from you in how to be positive or negative, in thought and action, and sometimes in spite of your best efforts, they do not think as you think and bring disappointment and anxiety into your heart.

"Oh, I tried to bring my child up well, but I failed!"

Responsibilities

But my friends, everyone has to learn, and the whole system must move forward and not back into the dark ages. There has to be a sublime truth – an initial fact that will capture and hold the spirit within, to guard against any negativity. To guard against allowing free will to move into the negative zone of harm and destruction. For where negativity loves best, is within harm and destruction, combat and fear. This negativity can spread through your mind by your thoughts, of how you may or may not be able to control your offspring. How you can make them think the way you do and not have a mind of their own.

It is important for every individual to accept his or her free will, to be aware of their personal responsibilities to everyone, ever mindful and searching for purer truths. There *is* such a will, there can be such strength given and received by the whole of the human spirit. You are tested repeatedly, to see if you have the inner resolve, to bring forward the positivity of love, and the enchantment of balance and harmony. Not to blend with the fairies my friend, but to move instinctively through your world. To move and refresh other minds, and yes – also those who may not think as you think!

It is better to have a field full of dancers, than a field with only one dancer and many mourners carrying their crosses of woe and foreboding. You can all join the happy field of life, you can all witness it; the truth is there, it is bountiful and harmonious. The love you have is yours. You may give it freely and openly, it will never run out so long as your thought is pure and you are at one with your spirit.

We are not trying to be high and mighty with you; we are merely at your service. With only love and peace in our hearts, with only the highest vibration that we may bring, to aid, guide, and nurture you along your pathway. We do not wish to appear holy or righteous, or make your material dreams come true, but to assist you in the gaining of balance and harmony of your inner spirit, so that you may have a long and happy existence.

All is here through love and a greater understanding and awareness of spirit that we entrust to our fellows here upon the earth plane, which can be passed from generation to generation. Not covered up in religious dogma, but just plain and simple truth.

Action of right or wrongdoing
That occurs in any state of being
Make their mark upon the owner
And can never be scrubbed out
They are as a sign
To enlist the help of others
Not in anger but in peace

So put away your truth swords
They are not needed today
It is truth who needs a friend
Like sincerity and care
Who beckon you make your walk
To further advance with evidence
That truth can be many shades
And dwell in many houses

Understanding Affliction

You all have some very difficult problems to deal with on the physical plane. You are embedded in the pro's and con's of life, as you toil in the hot sun or the freezing rain, trying to get to grips with your lives and battling with the world on which you live.

Battling with yourselves too, for many of you seem to think that you have become a prisoner locked in a body you do not wish to have, and some of those bodies do not work too well.

Friends, it is not that they are made of poorer quality materials, and it is only a deformity in a way of thinking, in how it is viewed. Still, you may wonder how God can allow this. How spirit can let me suffer in this way? It is a very difficult question, and one that requires care and love to answer.

Whether or not you have some kind of affliction is not a lottery and you were not cursed with it. It may be a genetic twist. It may be that the balance was not quite right, but it was not brought about on purpose as some sort of punishment. You are not a walking advert. You are not a gift bestowed upon others so that they may learn by your mistake. No, it is just that the physical body has a twist or the mental process is impaired or different. My friend, it is not that you are a scar upon humanity and it is not that you are unwanted or unloved. You are not a lesson to us all. You are just you … and you are a beautiful spirit.

Perhaps you cannot do all of those things that are models of life. You have another model, you have a different concept, and so it is with all who are on your side of life, and on our side of life. We still have different concepts and ideas as to what life is about, but that does not detract from the basic truths and facts. That you, the entire life energy force and me, are all a part of God, and you are not tainted because you have an affliction.

However, because you have had to endure it for your life I am sure you do not feel this way, and we understand your feelings, for we do not wear your shoes – we are not walking your path.

The compassion that spirit has for all on your side of life, no matter what they go through, is of the very highest. Whether an affliction is by accident or by some genetic circumstance it makes little difference, for you could still bring the essence of your spirit into the hearts and minds of others. Even if you feel you are the ugliest thing that walked the planet upon which you live, you can instill a positive response as you face your world, as you try to grapple with your complexes and situation.

Every person must try to achieve a balance that is within their scope, within their capacity, but you need to stretch the mind. You need to get the brain/mind function working in harmony together, so that the brain can solicit things to be put into the mind, for certain processes of work and activity of information mapping. For at the moment of transition to our side, the mind is the one that leaves, and everything you have processed along your way is stored within there. You must understand that there are so many layers of the mind. Not just conscious and sub-conscious, there are many in between also, many layers where you can store limitless amounts of information.

There is a duality of purpose between the progress of the mental and the physical body, and also of the purpose and progress of the spirit, which has made that journey. The spirit is always searching for what glimmer of truth can be perceived and understood by the mind to which it is attached. You see, although one may have little awareness of their physical body, the mind may well be active, and because the mind transfers to the soul (the spirit that is you) upon passing to our side, so much can still be gained from that journey.

At the end of the day, it does not matter what your level of intelligence is, because spirit is for everyone and higher learning can be a process of upliftment for the mind. However, it can also be dullness; it can stifle if taken in the wrong manner. It can be like taking a pill for a headache or taking the whole bottle. The brain can be swamped with information of a certain given subject so that there is very little room for anything else, including any other thought or gift towards humanity. The problem can be that you subjugate everything else for it if you are not careful, but you can balance this with seeking inner quality, with inner strength and inner harmony.

It may be possible for others who do not suffer in the way, in which the few do, to understand a little more by example, through love, help, guidance, and understanding. By taking a little more time to appreciate the enormity of one's own life, and how everyone has to cope with their day-to-day living. It may not be good enough to try to put yourself in anyone else's shoes, for you cannot contemplate any other person's viewpoint or understanding of how they see something. You can only see as close as you can get; a proximity of a picture, but you will never see exactly the same picture and it would be folly to try.

Understanding is a different matter, and you might come to do that by placing yourself at their disposal, by placing yourself in service of the one that you are trying to help. Only then may you be able to see glimpses of the world through their eyes as you interact with it. Through small windows, you may see little glimpses of that spirit within. You may see little pieces of the character and form a closer understanding of the wants and needs of others. Not by precondition, but by giving wholly and gently – in the name of love.

> We may by our word and action
> Try to make a difference
> Come as the truth swords that stand and guard
> We can pull at the harmony veils
> To see how we make judgments
> By what we see as different and not as we are
>
> We can try again and again
> And still fail to notice
> Those inner qualities that we lack
> Like foundation stones missing
> From our essential walls
> That hinder our freedom
> And right for our spirits to grow
>
> We deliver these consequences in bags and boxes
> We shout our domain and fence and ring
> Stamping our mark upon the skin
> Still unyielding in the light

Changing Your Inner Vision

I suppose there are many on your side of life who would wonder why you should wish to follow this path, or why anyone should wish to 'change their lot,' as it were. Most have a set routine and day-to-day living becomes familiar, safe, and repetitive. Maybe it is getting up late on a Sunday morning and reading the paper, mowing the grass if the weather is fine, and then going to work for the rest of the week. Perhaps it is normal to be thinking about the next item of luxury to save up for, or planning the next holiday.

How intricate your lives are. All jostling for position whilst perhaps wishing to be seen to be more adaptable or more knowledgeable about a particular thing. Plus, all of your life stories are slightly different, the things that interest you, which draw your attention. Whether you drink or whether you smoke or use other recreational facilities that are available to you, you are all individual.

Except, do you still have your freedom really? To do what you wish to do. Yes, you may be very comfortable; you are able to slouch in your easy chair, go to the gym or swimming when you want, and if you feel you are living your life to the full, then fine. Though, are there any wonders in your life? Are there any new borders that you may cross, other than snowboarding down a mountainside perhaps, or jumping out of airplanes?

Yes, there are many physical things that you may experience; new and exciting journeys that you may take. However, the one place you possibly have not journeyed to of late is that of the mind. Many on your side of life, I suspect, would not have any inclination to go there – scary stuff perhaps. Maybe they would not know how, or even have any notion of the possibilities of what there is still unexplored.

The spirit inhabits a body that you get to know during your time of physical life, like reading a map. Your mind is a very different thing. You see your mind as a tool to use for calculation, in working out the many difficult problems that you have to embrace in daily life, so you may move forward in your field of existence. But, there are many, many other doors within the mind that you have not yet opened, even though some of you seem to be searching it in order to find them.

Some doors are not obvious; some of them are not shown. They are not made available to you unless you are willing to do some work, and that means putting yourself in the right texture, within the right feeling.

Now, that may be a difficult concept to grasp, for it intimates that the mind within the brain is just that.

Perhaps you have always thought: "Oh yes, it's in this compartment a few inches from my eyelids, and that part is where I think this, and that bit on the other side is where these particular feelings come from."

However, it is not like that. I am sorry to disappoint you clinicians, but it is not. It may be that areas of the brain have certain facilities, but the brain has little to do with the

Changing Your Inner Vision

mind. The brain is just merely your tool for accessing and you train it. Then with it, you are able to do all manner of things; judgment, distance, all sorts in every situation that you have a dealing hand in. But there are matters that are separate, that are without the need for, or that require other parts of the body. You can use your mind, and your mind can actually have a free will of its own.

You may use it to embrace the spirit within, as a kind of staircase to it. You may have a happy life and you can access many things for yourself, but you can also go to many places without even having to leave your chair. You do not need a computer with incredible generated graphics to put you in a land of another existence that you have not experienced on your side of life. You have not experienced it, either because you have not wished to or because you have not made the effort. Maybe you have not channeled your energies into the reason for going within.

Therefore, there is yet another completely new realm waiting for you to explore, where you will find it is not a place, but an energy and a life. A life that is you, and once you make contact you can speak to you. Lift your own receiver and you can speak within the mind, communicate with yourself. There is a whole myriad of dimensions that you are unaware of, and it is not mind-games; it is not trivial, neither is it fantasy. It is real, and I do not have to prove it because you may go there and prove it to yourself, and that is the challenge to everyone on your side of life.

You do not have to take my word, it is possible for you all to go within and explore who you are, to find the spirit that you are. The more you go within, the more you may sense, and then you may ask different questions about your life and how you live it.

You see, your life is not just about going about your daily tasks. 'Within' is something different, and not on the physical plane. You cannot stand on it, you cannot take it and put it in a box and market it so that people will buy it. Within is just you – the spirit that you are – magical and wonderful. Think for a moment, as you sit there you can go into a completely new world. You can sense, see, and feel your spirit, and realize that you the spirit, are something other than the physical being. You will begin to sense that you are, in fact, a spirit looking out from a physical body!

Welcome to your new plane of existence my friend. Welcome to your new feeling ... your new horizon to explore.

Do not misunderstand me, I do not mean you just go there for excitement. I am just trying to stress that there is another field of existence that is without you and within you at the same time. You can go to your spirit whenever you wish, and you may speak, feel, and dance with any facet of yourself. You may explore any mode of understanding; can sit in any garden and go there. You can choose a quiet moment, not for reflection of your life, but understanding and moving forward within it.

Reflection is just a lot of past circumstances, which are regurgitated for further digestion, for further empathy or negative strokes for your ego. You may wish to reinvent your image or other things of a personal nature, which you may not even want to accept or acknowledge about you.

I am not saying that you are all like that; I would not wish to presume so. Nature, man, and the very will of it, are as diverse, complex, and complicated as two grains of sand, so I would not presume at all to try to lump you all together. Therefore, it is a little difficult speaking here and saying things that will encompass everyone.

This is why we come day after day, to bring to light the different twists and turns upon why and how you may progress. We come to help you understand that by exploring your inner-self you may come to know your spirit, and this is why we do this work. You may well find what you were looking for, and that it was right under your nose all of the time. It was right there for your life to experience, for you to become the gatherer, instead of a parcel on the doorstep.

> If we assume those who lead us
> Speak high words
> Why is it that we do not elect those
> Who write them

The Power of Prayer

Every day you begin anew and every day is a question, which can be trivial and mundane or awe-inspiring. When asked in the right manner, you may receive answers back to broaden your mind. Some answers you get might shrink it, and some may make no sense whatsoever, for we are still dealing with the act of freewill and it is still your decision as to whether to accept or not.

There you are, you are making your own judgment, but a judgment of what?

As you look back through your life, do you find you have made a succession of ill judgments and bad timings? Did you fight causes that were not there or that were not yours? Perhaps you had ideals of a certain nature, which were beaten out of you; or that you just lost through lack of want, through a lack of desire to achieve that particular journey. The good things that can happen, the little trips into paradise can seem awesomely simple to make whilst you see other people making them.

So here we are now, some time later down the road of discontent, and as you observe your friends and relatives, as you see the world impacting upon their lives, you notice how life changes and affects them. The pain and suffering you have been through and the impact it has had on your life may not be so much you may think, when some have such an awful time.

It is all of these things that stir the inner feelings of love. It is not charity, it is love – service. When you see someone else having such an awful time in their life, even if it is something you see on the television, you feel the love deep within flowing from you to that situation and you feel hopelessness at not being able to help.

However, you can still become involved. You can send thoughts out through the airwaves – upon the ether. Oh yes, it does work, the power of prayer is magnificent. People say that man has been praying for thousands of years for peace and love to come, and such prayers have been answered my friend, for if it were not so, you would not have some of the peace that you have now. If it were not so, you would have much more violence than you have now, and much more destruction.

There is more gained through the power of thought and more love given to each other than your world dreams of, and without it you would be less than animals in the desert. Without prayer, you would not be as loving and as sympathetic as you are, and would only know disharmony and negativity. So do not say that the power of prayer is wasted or does not exist, for it is evident all around.

You see, the fact that you possibly cannot save a particular person's life here on your earth plane, is perhaps because it is their time to make their transition – but you cannot say that prayer does not work. It may be that you are praying for the wrong thing, for the wrong reasons. Perhaps you should be praying that they pass in an easier manner than they might have, or that they may live on to understand what their life journey has been about. Make your prayer to that person, to that spirit, and not for you to keep them here in your world unnecessarily, delaying their journey.

When you pray for someone who is sick, the reason should not only be that you want him or her to get better. If they should be gravely ill and about to pass at any time, instead of hanging on to your own selfish cause, through your own fears of "please do not leave me," bless them for their journey. You must realize that no one leaves anyone. You have your journey here upon the earth plane, and we are right next to you having our journey and interacting with you.

Yes, well that is fine for people with particular gifts or mediumistic talent, you may say. No, every one of you can feel when a loved-one who has passed draws close; your parents, brother, sister, partner or friend, you can all feel it. You just do not acknowledge it for you have become desensitized, and that is your journey of discovery; it is part of your plan to rejuvenate yourself and regenerate those sensitivities, which are lost.

There is so much you can do for yourself. You do not have to wallow in fear and self-pity, and you do not have to cry through the nights of sleepless love. You do not have to wish things for God to do that God cannot, neither do you have to put pressure on yourself to complete tasks that you cannot fulfill.

You can learn to love. You can learn to be at peace and to aid and assist others. You could make your journey so much simpler if you wish it, and you can cease the angst that you feel and the terror you feel about what is to come. There is no terror.

It is true friends that many people on your side of life may be seen to pass in the most unpleasant manner, but it is unwise to dwell upon exactly how a person passes. For if you believe death is the final outcome and you will then be no more, never again to sense and shine out as a beacon, then you may become locked within that moment of passing.

Do you see that mentally you almost revisit that place of moment every time you close your eyes or maybe hear specific music? This can then become a system of torment for you, because it is revisited again and again, and not released. It does no good for the spirit of the one who has passed, for your mortification at their passing is felt on all sides of life. It does not mean to say friends that you love them any less if you let them go. If anything, you love them more by releasing them, in wishing them well upon their journey of light.

You must come to terms with these important facts of life and how everything works. Sometimes it is for reasons too complex for your mind to understand, and by saying this, I am not being condescending. It is why you need to relax within the situation that you are in, and try to make progress upon your understanding. Of how life is to you now. Not how it seemed to you in the days when you began your searching ideals, when you began to evaluate your inner most feelings. For feelings change – they grow and blossom like the flowers you are.

One may ask what is prayer
That does not exist anywhere else
The answer comes
To those who give energy in love
Each simple thought we have
Is as sacred as any other
When we ask the ultimate source to listen
Each measured step and word of asking
Is as blessed from any lips
When we seek ourselves in mindful mantra
And speak our soul to those who hear
We join all worlds in greater union
So clear ... so clear

When filled with love or feeling empty
And we happen upon a door of light
Seek not for self, seek not for grievance
But be pure in thought and right
With love you give in asking
With love comes back ten fold
The power of prayer unbending
The power to lift and heal
Yea, these are sacred moments
Your spirit, you, and I
When little words are uttered
Do not cry ... do not cry

Prayer is for courage
Set free from pain and ease
All life that turns upon its head
You are free little bird, you are free

Checks and Balances

Although we speak about the ills and depravations that man inherits from one another, we are not speaking from a lofty position. Your decision, your free will is there for you to roam as you would wish, and it is up to the structure and the laws within your society whether to place restraints upon individuals who would do harm or cast fear to others. It is not for spirit to speak out, other than to say that it is up to you in your life to learn your path and your journey, to become a better spirit, to be a better human being. If you cannot fathom or deal with the question of spirit, then at least you can be within the involvement of love from your side. It is not really much to ask in order to improve your own destiny.

In the spirit realm the choices are far more profound, as they are more carefully weighed and do not involve the negative aspect as much as on your side of life. Oh yes, we do still experience negativity from time to time; fellow spirit travelers on our side of life can develop problems, or may arrive with difficulties from your side, which all have to be treated and overcome. We cannot say that we are all sweetness and light either, for there are many who wish to continue their, shall we say, earthly ways, and these may be kept at arms length by the rest of us.

We cannot say that travel is always as difficult as you are presently finding it though, for it is much easier when you are on our side of life, more beneficial and more rewarding. However, what we do say is that you must atone for the ills you may have caused, for the effect that you may give your fellow travelers and those of the future. Checks and balances for your actions need to be made, so that you the spirit, even if you have gone through your entire physical life without recognizing your real existence, may still move forward. Progress is open for all.

When we speak on concerns of your desire towards the planet and towards each other, we hope this brings out the harmony within you. That you bring out these feelings, gently coaxing if necessary, for the standard and length of your lives may depend upon it. The manner in which you live will depend upon it. It is not too late for you to learn to share and be more caring to each other.

If you are the type of person who disregards other people (even if you do not admit it), it is not a weakness or a backward step to be gentle or to show love. To gather someone in your arms and say: "I'm sorry."

There is no real joy in control over another. It is only in your mind, and that mind has a distorted perspective on reality. It is so much kinder to let freedom move you forward in partnership with a helping hand, so that all may become positive – if this is your wish.

How can we cause damage
To those who can offer us
So much in another aspect of life
For every action we make now
We will revisit upon the return journey
When we must shake the hand
Of those who wrong us
And whom we have disfavored

May those avenues you seek to address
And all those little bits of life
You could not fit in your pocket
Be the treasures you may wear
As illuminations
So people may see all of you
From time to time

Question of Access

It is your undertaking to fulfill the promises to restore and acknowledge the love that is within you. To carry out the agreement to reach for a higher knowing and understanding and experience a deeper and more tender love. This is often very difficult, for it takes a much greater depth than you may have previously thought possible within your understanding. Time after time, you may have believed you had reached it, only to find another corner or hurdle that you must negotiate. That there is still a little more thread to grasp, in order to secure a roundness of understanding of a particular aspect and desire that you feel within.

It is your divine right to travel within your time frame with no parameters of thought to be excluded, with no events upon your physical reality to be curtailed. For you are here to experience life on the physical level, but all of the senses you have been given are not yet realized. Therefore, you need to strive to find a way through the knitted pathway of lies, doubt, and fear. You need to find the path, so you may travel in your understanding and continue your search for a greater abundance of it.

You can hear my words now, because we are able to communicate on a slightly different level, within a different vibration and generation of love. This is to show you the capability that is possible. We do this so that you can become aware of other things, which are not set in black and white before your eyes. So that you may look further than the tree in the distance: to look within the space around it, above it and below it, to look beyond and see a different horizon – a different perspective.

The more you look within your own horizon, within your own life; you will draw greater detail and gain a greater unfoldment of knowledge within your existence on your physical plane. Perhaps it may not be instant recollection, but it all goes to make up further evaluation and detail, a growing bundle of sincerity, honesty, love, and emotion.

My friends, these are the things you need to remember and all of the lies, doubts and deceits, you need to throw away, and not let them continue with you on your journey. This will help you to blossom and grow. To realize the full assets within your emotional and mental capabilities, and enable you to bring them forth. Not just in times of need for others, but also for yourself. You can draw upon the energies of the universe of the eternal spirit. You can draw upon those energies in times of need, and there is no doubt that as you journey, your needs become apparent.

Do not feel afraid that you take something for yourself. This is your right. Why not? Never feel you have not earned the right to fully experience love, emotion, and compassion. Everyone upon your side of life has the right to allow these feelings to flow through them, to assist in overcoming the hurdles of life; to rise and make good those events that you believe are undone.

Furthermore, the experiences that you would rather forget; the negatives, they need to be buried. You can no longer afford or need to take them around with you. If you

Question of Access

can discard them, you will find that although those around you may appear grey and distant, your outlook can change, regardless of whether people tell you otherwise.

Now, I know this is all very well for me to offer you advice, for I am not enduring your side of life as you are and you have a different picture to paint, as everyone does. You all have different sized hurdles and they are all relative to your own individual set of problems. It is a bit like going up a hill that seems endless. From a distance, you thought the hill looked very low and rolling, but when you actually get there, you find rocks and boulders that you had not seen or anticipated, and you find that you did not bring the right equipment with you in order to climb them. Sometimes, it may feel like you have been set down upon your side of life with no tools with which to make your journey; that you are as helpless as a babe, there for the lions to eat.

God that you are, the spirit that you are within, could not possibly allow such folly to exist. The very fact that you are spirit, that you make your journey and that God is within you, proves that you are actually very well equipped.
However, what you need to learn is how to access it, how to access yourself, so that you may be able to grow into a better specimen …into a kinder and more open being of light.

Glorious in thy hand my friend
Do not fret all is there for you
Your past will no longer
Dominate your sky
It will finally say goodnight
All those bad memories
Not forgotten but let go
And you will walk
With whom you wish
In the summer sun

Vibration

There is no necessity for glumness or tear's of sorrow at a loved-one's passing, for they are as close as you are to these words now. Close enough, so that the vibration of that person can be felt on your side of the physical plane, and physical contact can be made once again.

Now, this is quite interesting, because you do not notice that you vibrate, for within the physical plane your vibration seems to be dulled. Indeed, it is so much slower than the vibration on our side of life. This is why you need to meditate, for with practice you will be able to bring you and your mind within the confines and realities of which you exist, to bring your vibration up to speed, as it were. When you do this you are not aware of the changes, but they occur nonetheless, thus enabling you to blend within the harmonic balance of the planet.

This should instill much joy within you, as you are hopefully beginning to understand how uplifted you may be and what this experience feels like. Not just an inner calm, but a sense of wonderment, at the sheer magnitude of all of those ramifications that result from it. That here you are upon a physical plane, thinking this is all there is, and then you begin to experience the feelings and the physical sensations about your body, as spirit make contact with you.

It is not wishful thinking on your part, but a universal need to be able to contact each other. To seek each other out, in order to give help and sustenance, to touch each other's lives and be of benefit to each other. We may all be in different realms of light, but we are all on this fine journey. We are all rowing the same boat, but on different decks, on different levels, and occasionally we bump into each other on the stairs.

The vibration you create is so important, because it is this that gives you the harmonic balance throughout your world. It is why, when someone does any damage however slight, or has ill feeling or ill will towards another, it sends vibrations all the way through and it is felt by everyone, knowingly or not. If you were attuned to it you may feel it and recognize it for what it is, for you are a part of the whole.

You can tell when negativity fields surround you and attack you, for when you encounter it the vibrational signals that you emit change quite drastically. You all reflect each other; you all vibrate from each other's feelings, emotions, and events. All events. Not just within your sphere of light friends, but within the whole of your planet. All of those circumstances will have an effect upon you.

Negative events set up large fields of negative energy, which can either drift or be sent very fast, and telepathic negativity can be almost instantaneous. You may wonder why these things can happen. Well, these situations are just a product of the age you are living in now, and it is time to try to gather yourselves up and proceed forward in light and knowledge, with an awareness of the truth.

There are so many opportunities for you to grow. You can never say to spirit that you have not been lucky to experience being in touch with the spirit that you are, or with we, from spirit around you – for you all can. We can

Vibration

all communicate in many ways, it is not difficult, for if it were difficult it would be for the privilege of the few and that is not what spirit is about. It is about close harmony, love, and attention, about a realization of existing truths and of further wisdom's and knowledge, to bring you up and along the pathway of your own success.

You do not have to have a large income to be happy as you have a complete storehouse of treasures within you. We have an even larger one waiting, and as you open your eyes and begin to reach out with your mind and become in contact with your spirit, then those treasures may be illuminated to you. Not sought out by you though, for it would not involve any kind of humanity's greed, but you will receive them one at a time, as an allotted course of the unfolding within; when the mind acceptance begins to take shape.

Consequently, within the spirit that you are, through the relationship you form within the spirit light, you become aware and accustomed to your inalienable rights as a fellow spirit traveler, to perceive and to journey where you wish. Your only credentials, your passport if you like, is that you have and generate love within you, to be mixed with all of that within the cosmic realms surrounding you, and all of that love you experience is just a small fraction of the whole.

Show love – and not just in times of tragedy, but in moments of great joy, for greater unfoldment of your heart and mind within the nature spirit that you are. Lift your vibration for the benefit of each other. You may take and draw as much as you wish, for the more you understand the more you will automatically give back. Therefore, you may take as much as you like, for you can never take it all. Once you are open and within the harmony house of spirit, you will always be giving back.

Take care with the harmony
You would invite upon your being
Not to stride upon others lives
Through lack of care and vision
Make the right play
Sing out with the greatest voice
For goodness

Protection

When you wish to protect yourself upon the physical world, you have the use of certain moves and ways of combat or artistry in which to defend yourself against foes that are seen. However, what about those adversaries and unwanted gifts of people, which are directed at you in the form of negative thoughts and feelings?

You can tell when these come to strike at you as you can feel them through your auric field and they may make you ill. Sometimes, they may even confine you to bed if you are particularly sensitive. They are like pulses of negative energy, which is in fact, what they are. They will not really hurt you in the same way as someone physically attacking you, but they may bring with them much negative energy force from the deliverer.

What you can do is you can use your mind and your auric field to protect yourself. You can just think yourself into a bubble. Imagine that you are within wonderful petrol colors; construct it all the way around yourself so you are just floating in it.

Except, if the mental missiles that are being hurled at you are particularly sharp, they may go through this, so you may need to construct a different mechanism, one of mirrors. Then once again using the mind as a tool to do this, imagine you are completely surrounded by mirrors that will deflect these undesirable thoughts and feelings.

There is, of course, the area of the solar plexus, which can be covered by means of the hand or of thought. You may also ask of spirit – you may ask your doorkeeper and your guides in a prayer to protect you.

You may ask the aspect of God within you to protect you. After all, you are a part of the eternal life force, and you may call upon that power at any time when you are in need, when the need is sincere and just.

> We sit beneath the thought tree
> We gather the kernels
> As they land upon our reality
> We break them open
> And we listen to their content
> They dissolve within our minds
> Their wings accelerating our rate of intent
> Brandishing our love as we climb
> To ever-greater harmony and knowledge
> The purest thoughts we pat and brave
> Brave charms that stand as lanterns
> To the love we have within us
> They are bounteous in motion
> Unrivalled in clarity
> They bring us within sight
> Of our God

Structure of Thought

No matter what we believe, no matter what we think we know, there is always so much more. Every facet of your thinking encompasses other facets of other people's thinking, including generations of spirit thought. All of these thought processes are journeys made upon the ether within the physical world on which you live. Information is there from countless learning before, so as you graze within the valley of learning you may from time to time pick up little gems of wisdom. Like flowers in a field. Just pick them up and take in their beauty; fully understanding their richness of color, scent, or warmth, brought into your being, so you too may appreciate the relevance of it within your life.

There are many things you will encounter upon your journey with which you may not agree. These disagreements must be rationalized, because they are the personal result of your journey within your own process of learning. The disagreement that you may have is with someone else's journey and process of learning, for they will not always match. You all have free will and that is what free will means. You may go to any field you wish. There are no fences or barriers within the fields that you may not visit. This is the purpose of free will and it is the only true free will you will experience.

It may take some effort of thought and a certain courage on your part, but that is the secret my friends. Each part of all understandings given and received have to be analyzed most carefully before it is accepted or not. You must make decisions upon and within your life that affect the respect you have for each structure of thought you come across. The thought processes and ideologies, of which I speak about, are all possible ways forward for many other individual spirit travelers having an earthly journey. You simply cannot say that one is right and one is wrong for they are individual aspects of the journey. Therefore, you may wonder how you might come to any sort of decision.

You have many religions, many thought structures concerning how and why you and the universe exist. How and why may God exist within you ... how can this be? What if I do not want God in me? There are many that do not wish to be an aspect of God – who would be horrified at the mere thought of it, and that is how different the spirit journey can be my friends. You must learn to have a large degree of tolerance – tolerance of all manner of people's way.

This does not mean to say you just go and think that whatever rubbish comes into your head is fact. Except, how then do you differentiate the rubbish from fact, if we say everyone's thought is their own and everyone's right to make their journey is, as they will? How can there be any order within this chaos, and how can there rise from such chaos, any wish or regard for higher thought, or any wish for a greater abundance of knowledge? There are so many ideologies, thought patterns and processes, that it is difficult to disseminate one from another, so how do you separate the many paths and choices and decide which is right for you?

Well, you have to be able to dissect information and take out the parts you feel sit comfortably within your own framework. You have grown using this form of learning. You have begun to build up your own individual character and personality, for there was plenty of information you could have accepted, but you will have rejected it.

Then how have you come to make the choices that you have? Because at the moment of decision, something within you has become alight. It shows you a pathway of thought that you may love or reject, love and reject, love and reject. Those parts that you have taken into your heart, which you have fully accepted into the mind, are those that fit right for you. They are so obviously your truths, for they perfectly fill the spaces that were there. They become your sublime truths by which you can live your life, and are the reason for your existence. Because of their very nature they shine out from all of the rest of the information that comes to you; you are able to pick them out and blow off the debris.

You maybe had some patterns of thought or ways of being from much earlier on in your life and suddenly, it may be twenty, thirty, or forty years after you were born, that your whole thinking pattern changes. You think in a completely different way. You drop all of the previous information and take on a completely new perspective and thought process. How do we know whether these milestones are of benefit, are of clarity, and focus of the mind and of the spirit? How do we know these are real truths that will provide progress within your learning, and not something else to take you off onto another track, or be detrimental to your progress?

You can only see how it feels deep within, within the spirit that you are. That, my friend, is why it is so important that you sit in meditation and go within. That is why it is so crucial to your development of life – that you sit whenever you can. If you have just twenty minutes of your time out of all of those twenty four hours that makes a day, just twenty minutes set aside for you to be with your spirit or with your friends in spirit, then a different structure of thought may be impressed upon you.

It will help you to conduct your life for the better and maybe then, you might not take on so much of the woolly-headedness of many of your contemporaries. You may become the spirit, feeling the spirit. Not dressing up in fine clothes, but seeing the true nature of the spirit within. You may then find that your attitude can change. Your whole demeanor may become more relaxed and you may reach out instead of shrinking back. You may reach out for the hand of God that exists with you and for you, and that you are a part of.

You have some questions
We have answers
Questions bring further to the consciousness
Different avenues of paths
Down which memory and chance may dwindle
Into one pure light thought
That reason has come to stay

Each answer can become either a sword
For its rightful practice
Or a dungeon of the mind
To sink into obscurity and loss
Create the right thoughts
And answers will be given

In all form you look
Are the answers of the universe
But do not take them for granted
Some may only appear once in a while
And you may lose their meaning
If not respected in the greatest light

Knowing Yourself

We have noticed that people have great problems in taking on new ideas and show much reluctance with letting go of old concept – something, which holds them back in their progression. It seems that man's intention is for growth if possible, but at the moment unfortunately, it is always seen to be in the material manner, although we do believe this will change as people progress with their spiritual path. It is like a star being born if you like, and the old viewpoints once held will begin to crumble away.

Nevertheless, those on your side of life do hang on relentlessly to matters of the past. All of those memories and ill judgments, doubts, fears, and anxieties, they hang around the necks of man like an abhorrent noose. The fear of failure, instilled perhaps by parents, teachers and peers, whatever – all of that negativity that man has bestowed upon himself.

It is possible to relinquish some of these. You do not have to endure the memory of your anger that you felt last week, going over and over it in your mind. Or reliving a decision you once made, which you now think was ill timed or disastrous. This, of course, may also apply to the loss of a loved one from your side of life. It is a similar situation, because your negative grief structure has been linked with fear, and unless you are able to turn that fear into positive energy, you will not make a change within you.

Now, I know we have spoken about fear and doubt many times before, but it seems to be that man is so intent on hanging onto it; like fur in a kettle, it seems impossible to chip it all off. You have maybe gone throughout your whole life fighting with it. Fighting with your past. Maybe even fighting with your parents past – even the past of your country. However, the past can be a bed of negativity that stretches and engulfs everyone, that 'it' has a tragic past. For some reason, there appears to be this strong empathy within a population for a tragic past event, which seems to bond and unite people together.

Many upon your side, use their fear and accumulated negativity from their past as a way of doing nothing. But all of you can do something to remove yourself from it and to guard against future occurrences. You can move forward with trust and guidance from within. It is not something that you observe in someone else. Forget how anyone else is doing and how you would wish to emulate that person. It is the old pedestal trick.

You have to be your own person, not someone else's, and you can gently remove all of those misguided shackles of time that you have experienced – those fields of woe. It does not mean to say you become uncaring or unthinking, or that you may become callous and hardened to feeling. Every one of those life experiences, including the mistakes, have all been there for your growth and learning.

You do not need to be constantly reminded of how to spell a word you learnt many years ago. You do not have to keep going over it, for it is deep within you. Likewise, you do not need to keep being reminded of your errors in such a physical way. They can be put in the distant memory box and you can shut the lid and turn the key – gone!

You see, the negative vibration you receive from it is a source of recurring damage. It is something, which is not only keeping you in the position you are in, in your life, but is also having an impact upon how you then perceive new thoughts. Because when you have a new thought coming in, there is negative fear and doubt looking at it also, so you will see everything in a different perspective.

Once you have taken all your past fears and doubts away, then how you perceive new ideas, are just you and the idea. You will be unclouded, and have a clear aspect from your window of life in which to study the universe, your surroundings, and yourself – your spirit and I. You will be able to see how it all fits and you will be brighter and happier for not having such a heavy load to carry.

Grieving and Negativity

When you reflect on the past, you will often remember situations of deep sorrow and anguish over which you had no control. You may even still have great difficulty many years later, in overcoming such stress and trauma. It could be an accident of a very personal nature or almost anything. Situations that are hard to deal with at the best of times can actually turn your life and your mind inside out.

Thankfully, there are many fellow travelers on your side of life who do a lot of work in trying to alleviate these problems. However, much of it is only helpful in a certain way, and can sometimes, only be taken as far as finances will allow. For instance, you may be having counseling for years without success, for it might not necessarily be the path for you to take, in order to relinquish your past for a brighter tomorrow and for a more self-respectful now.

In relation to parents who have lost a young child, the grieving may go on for many years, for the love bond is so strong, they will never-ever forget. And why should they, you may say? But friends, there are ways of lessening the pain that you carry with you. Yes, time does make all the difference, but not every difference – not every difference is taken care of. Very often, after the real pain and anguish of the moment subsides, the dullness sinks in, and it can be very difficult to maneuver yourself around or to alleviate your pain in any way. This negative situation can actually drag on for years and years, without respite or any hope of it ever being resolved.

Another example may be a set of parents losing an older child. They may have raised this child for eighteen, twenty, or thirty years, loving, and nurturing them. The pain through some devastating act, can never be lessened, never taken away – the room a shrine to memory and life. They yearn to hear their voice, to feel their presence and the touch of their physical form again. Yearned for beyond comprehension and any mark of sanity some may say. It is the sense of finality, of the loss, a foreboding that those times can never be regained.

There are many instances as you look back over your own lives, of people with whom you associated. Perhaps they were very good friends, lovers, or whatever, and all of those characters fulfilled your life and moment. You were a witness to each other's journey here upon the physical plane.

The purpose of this is that all of those feelings and records of love, which were and are, held within each and every one of us, are part of your make up now. They are a part of who and how you are now, and your *now* does not have to totally represent someone else's life, a loved one who had passed. The memory is nonetheless if you go through less pain. You do not have to cherish the pain; your sorrow will not reflect a deeper hue for having been through such pain and distress. The love will not ever disappear, for love is always with you, but the negativity

Grieving and Negativity

that carries on through and within your life, is the candle that keeps the pain burning.

Love does so much better without the negative aspect devoted to the past. Love is not something retrospective, love is fulfilling now. Every moment of your life can be involved and can experience the beauty of love, and it does not make you a lesser person to be able to move forward from a given place or event in time. You can always take the first step and the first step is always the hardest step to take, but you must have the realization within you that you are able to move forward. Just as the sun moves across the sky, each moment that passes does not reflect that you are uncaring for not remembering. It reflects that you are stronger for the knowing of that person. You owe it to the memory, and you owe it to all of those who are around you now, in the present time, to move on with your life tasks ahead.

The same applies for almost every event within your life. You do not have to forget, but you can move with a greater respect for all that is living around you now. Then all of those pleasures, feelings and senses, new and aspiring may fulfill your life, without guilt and fear of negativity encroaching upon you again. You may move on and still allow yourself to reflect from time to time. This does not mean that you have forgotten, but rather that such things are now in your past. Your loved-ones who have come to our side of life would not wish you to dwell on their passing. In fact, it will actually hold them back, for they will feel compassion for your sorrow and your inability to let them go.

You can take your time, but in the meantime, what is happening within, is that you can become a stagnant spirit locked in a time past. Love can give you the courage to put the past gently to one side. You can remember every facet of it of course, as is your right, but do not neglect to accept new moments and stages of your own development within your life. There is so much more to enjoy, so much more to caress your heart and mind and your spirit. Do not let the negative ways win.

I know many doubts and fears have been rooted in your past. Maybe these have a large part to play in how you see and envisage your life and the way in which your past sometimes catches up with you. Some day, you too will move through the veil to our side of life, and to many this is the only certainty they can rely on, even if they believe it to be "The End." It would be a cruel God would it not, if this were the case, if you were to be just a slab of meat on a counter.

You, I, and every one of us on both sides of life, are very fortunate in that we are all a part of God. We are all on a journey through history, accepting challenges and new ideas, growing and nurturing our fellow companions who are walking with us. However, with foresight and within the acknowledgement of the spirit within us, we can gain greater steps in our development, both personal spirit contact and the development of that aspect of God that we are. They are many aspects of the same piece, and it can be applied to almost any part of your life.

To journey through life and not to ask questions is folly. To be uplifted from it is a desire and straightforward possibility of self-improvement, so you may become happy. You may think of times that have passed, where you have had the opportunity to share with each other, and these are blessings that will continue to be a part of your life if you allow yourself to attune to your senses. You will discover you are not completely who you thought you were. That you can be something better – someone better and you can improve everything within your life, regardless of physical circumstances.

We do not drift aimlessly across the landscape; we all have a journey and a job to do. Reflect only when it is necessary and you will not miss anything that is in front of you. However, dwell in the past and you will unfortunately miss everything, and you will not have had the trip you could have had. For this is just part of your learning curve, it is a gift from God that you are here, as we are all gifts. We all have to recognize that we are just different aspects of the same gift.

If truth were a labor to come to the mind
It would not exist
It is wrong pathways and ill planned courses
That are hard
The path of truth if the mind is clean
Is seldom difficult
It is decay, avarice and fear that draw barriers
Upon the path
That truth would wish to make

Truth or Consequence

We see you throwing your hands up in horror at the things mankind does to each other. We also see the state of bewilderment that exists with regards to just what people on your side of life view as fact. How is it possible that a single piece of information told by one could be so distorted in so many different ways by so many?

You could have a frog sitting on a table. It would appear that if you had a room full of people all looking at the frog, although they had all experienced the same frog, if they did not speak to each other, they would all have perceived within their minds a slightly different picture. So they had all seen a frog, but because of the fact they were each at a slightly different angle to the frog, it meant that they each saw a different aspect of it.

All of those ways and angles of seeing that vision are reality. Yet, what can happen is that certain recollections, facets of that reality can be left out in the mind, and you can then end up with a distorted picture. Then when passed on to another who never saw the picture in the first place, it is described distinctly differently from the original, and so it can go on, as it is handed down through the differences of opinion.

This is the manner in which religion has played a part on your side of life. For example, let us say it was written down perhaps two thousand years ago – yet maybe not that much of it at the actual time. That in fact, much of it was locked within the mind, and it was memory recollection that was written – then forgotten – and then a bit more written. Subsequently, as time passed, sections were translated into other languages, with parts of it conveniently left out and other bits put in, because it did not quite fit.

Of course, in the earlier days, most who walked the earth were not able to read or write. They were simple folk who just did whatever those who had been chosen to be close to God would tell them. Therefore, as history repeats itself or at least tries to, over and over, century upon century – it has kept many within ignorance of the truth.

This is not a criticism of a specific religious order. If indoctrination is what you wish to have, as we all know it is your choice, it is merely an observation. Though there are many ways of cracking a nut, and if you want to eat the nut, you do not smash it to pieces. You take the shell off very carefully to look at what is inside and then you can enjoy it.

People may wish to follow a particular set of beliefs, even a particular facet of a piece of work, and call it a religion. There are also many of those little elitist groups, which believe that they have the whole and total answer to the sum of the universe, plus one. Then how may there be progress among all of these misguided and thought provoking souls who walk the earth with you, but who seem to live in a completely different dimension? Where do we go from here? How can we uplift the spirit of man when he is so fixed in an idea of what life is? How can mankind live life in this way?

It is simple my friend – we can just let be, for it is everyone's choice to think in his or her way. I know it is hard to swallow friends, as you shake your head in disbelief at the things that man will do to man in the name of some abstract science or religion or other. Only, if you are not careful, this can also give you great angst within yourself, as to how all of these people may be reconciled with their truth. For in reconciliation there are the fruits of life, and one man's truth is not another's necessarily, regardless of its purity. They must reach their own conclusion in their own manner.

You can look on and merely observe. You can only live by your action, by your word and your deed. It is up to them and their spirit within them, through contact with each other, that they may begin to recognize some truths. You must stay calm; you must continue to be aware of the spirit that you are with a wish to carry yourself forward, so you may shine out within other people's reality. That they will notice there is something completely different about you they have not seen or experienced previously.

Many of you do not know truth; have never seen it. Your education has been pious and singular, unforgiving and relentless, and it shows you not the true spirit of the world upon which you live, but a bleak random reality. Nevertheless, a recollection and recognition of the truth may be instilled within each other as it is brought to the surface. It is not just by your hand, but by the hands of many. This will increase my friends, so fear not – it is not such an upward climb.

If a lie forms upon the thought
Within the consciousness
It creates an ellipse
From the physical form to the spirit

If it is uttered
Within the physical world
It creates misfortune
And adds to the strength of negativity

All lie
Is the seed of man's undoing
For if you look to the natural world
There is only truth to make your bed upon

Allowing Dysfunction

Your lives could certainly be much simpler if you did not pour fat onto the fire; emotionally, you could be so much more stable. It is not that you undergo what life throws at you, but what each of you throw at each other.

I suppose it is a part of life's rich tapestry. I also would not wish to preach morality to you and I am aware that we have talked about this before. However, it does seem to me that the more something is done, which is not right, the more it seems to be accepted as normal and so the more it is treated as an every day occurrence. The perpetrators of which, appear to be relieved of nothing and have no guilt. In every story, you have to look at both sides. What is caused by human action upon the victim, and upon the one who causes it? For dysfunction in one, causes dysfunction in the other – it is like a disease.

Now, I do not want to be negative. I am sure you are all aware of the distress that humanity's action upon each other leaves in all ways and instances, but it would appear almost as though your whole lives depend upon negative action. That is why it is so difficult to get it to turn around, for it is so prevalent. It would appear almost impossible nowadays, for you to go through even a third of your lives without encountering some physical violence or abuse in one form or another, and it does take many forms. For much of your life, you are forced to encounter daily mental abuse and torture. Mental abuse in the way in which you treat each other in negative will, and this is not good for your growth.

It is not good that you cannot see the true way. That you must remain within a book and not leave its pages. That you still feel you must remain dominated by those speeches and sentences, which were written so long ago. I can see you striving to get out, but the positive force that you can inhabit, is much more difficult to find when you are surrounded by so much negativity. You have had to evoke so many new laws to cope with it all, and yet it does not. People on your side of life are allowed to create havoc and to go on creating havoc, with no possibilities of ever curtailing their activities to the more positive forces that exist. They are allowed to continue unchecked, continuing to wreck more lives.

There has to be a time set aside for clear and pure thought to be brought within the auric field; to be brought within the life that you are, but first of all, you have to realize that you need this. There are very direct and matter-of-fact ways in which you can and should increase your moments for yourself, to attract positive forces. I am not saying that what I am suggesting is the only hand you may play. There are many ways in which you may still yourself and get to know who you are. Your life need not be as it is. It does not have to exist on the level it does, and you can rise above it. Not through being aloof and unconnected, but by being compassionate and in touch with self.

Unfortunately, a dilemma that faces humanity is that once they are awakened by their spirit they are sensitive, and all of that negativity surrounding each of you seems to become larger, for you recognize it more easily. You feel it as you encounter it through your daily life, and you begin to realize just how much of it there is and how little positive energy you actually generate.

However, negative forces are really very weak; it is only the power you give them that gives them strength, and you can all just turn it off.

You can turn on the positive force that is within you, and the negative will disengage itself from your life. You only have to get your positive broom out and sweep those negative forces away!

Well, that is the plan anyway, and I cannot reiterate it too strongly. It is your will, your motive and your action that will change your way, your attitude, and horizon. All of spirit are here to help in whatever way we can – you do not journey alone.

Healing Ring of Light

This is something that you can do to help yourself; if you are unwell, if you are suffering from the negative effects from others, or just feeling weighed down with life in general, you may aid your recovery with spirit healing.

Here is a method that you may employ with the help of we, in the spirit light, in the form of the Healing Ring of Light.

To begin with, you will need to obtain four matching candlesticks and candles, a comfortable chair, and a quiet room with enough space for the following.

Light the candles and as you put each candle down about a foot away from the chair – one in front, one at the back and one either side – say the following prayer aloud.

"To God, my highest guides and helpers
Please free me from this fear
Please free me from this bond
Please free me from this negativity
Surround me with love
Surround me with light
As I do in the physical
So do I in the spirit"

Sit on the chair, close your eyes, and quieten your mind as much as you can, and accept the healing from those who love and walk with you.

Afterwards, say a closing prayer or invocation giving thanks.

Before you start, decide how long you are going to sit for healing. It may be anything from ten minutes to half an hour and you may want to ask somebody to gently tap on your door making you aware when time is up, or set an alarm in another room if you are on your own.

This is something that you can all do for yourselves, and is very beneficial before going to bed, but it can also be done anytime you feel the need.

> Though negatives cry out to thee
> Be truthful and be free
> In mind be pure in love be sure
> Bring honesty to me
>
> Till all has past and love is cast
> Sing out your golden quest
> Through all of this prevailing sound
> Let right for you be blest

Love

Love is a very fine subject, but I wonder – do we really know what it is? Our experience of it is sometimes less than exciting and not very rewarding, for it can seem so fickle. Yet, there are so many different kinds of love. There are boundless possibilities of happiness that you may enjoy. However, with each other, it seems you gravitate towards one another one moment and then push each other away the next. Like opposite poles in a magnet. Love was never so fickle, and never is.

Still, would love only be the expression of one spirit traveler to another when having a human experience? Is love just a human experience? Something you just pick up and put down, as and when you feel the need. It appears to depend upon your mental outlook, and just how you envisage your life. Whether you are able or not to form attractions, bonds, and friendships, depends entirely upon your make-up and the make up of those around you. There are many whom you could never entertain the thought of being loved by or loving, for it may be that the fellow traveler appears so abhorrent in some way or another.

There are lessons in all things, and there are many different grades and kinds of love you may feel, experience or acquire knowledge of throughout your life. All of these different aspects you come to recognize one by one, as they take a hold of your very fiber. This will depend upon the resources you have and the way in which you are able to tap into the positive energy, as well as your ability to attune to the love energy you are experiencing.

Love relationships are all so different. Loved ones, friends, parents, children, animals, and all of the varying relationships in between. All are different modes of feeling, a vast array, like a cacophony of flowers in a vase. So many, that you could not fit all of those aspects into one place, or as a matter of fact, into one lifetime. It almost seems impossible that you could hold all of that love, or all of those different facets of what love is, and experience them in the time you have here on your side of life.

Indeed, you may not, for it entirely depends upon your journey. How long or how short you are here. It will also depend upon your life plan, and what you have to learn for your future further development, which will also depend very much on the type of relationships you have with your fellow travelers.

However, the first serious bond you have to make, to develop harmony, trust, and to learn to love … is you! You must learn to love yourself. To find within yourself those fruits that are you, which you exist to find. And this love you encounter is the first true relationship you can make, for you are recognizing the innocence within you that is part of God, and that love can be developed to encompass all things.

Having said that, I am not saying you should not have spent all of those formative years in the relationships with your parents, or whomsoever you came into contact with in your life journey up to this point. Nor that you should not

Love

have loved them in the way you did or do now. Love has many seeds and so much openness in which to gaze out upon varying different vistas. There are many different attitudes that you can learn with your spirit intact and in conscious involvement with you, your spirit self – your higher self.

When you become open to what is within you, you can say you have found a new form of love. Moreover, it does not matter what is on the outside, whether you have warts, or whether you have anything or nothing, you will always have something – your spirit. The love you feel for you within, can help you reflect, which in turn, enhances your will to change the way you are towards others. In so doing, the growth of love from within, via that aspect of God that you are, will find new harmonies and will settle most comfortably with those of your other fellow travelers who are around you.

These various aspects of love when delivered to their rightful place can help you to realize your greater potential, in your greater capability for progressing with strength and positive energy. The energy of love surpasses all. You cannot take it at will, as it has to be generated from within and it is from within that it comes.

If you are in a crowded room, you can very often feel love emanating from someone, the same as negativity does. Love is a means for forming balance and harmony between people. Many of you may not even realize from whence that emotion and feeling is generated. While part of your physical anatomy enables varying chemical processes to facilitate upliftment within on the physical level, the spirit that you are holds the key.

Learn to love who you are and do not accept the warts that may be on the inside, but try to progress within that journey, that you may discover new horizons and pleasure. There are so many journeys you can travel; you could go about your daily business on the physical side of life with an almost wondrous intent. Instead of that, you are sensitively blocking energies that are coming from others, which are generated towards you. You can accept everything that comes your way, various parts of it you may learn from, whilst others you may just lay to one side; we do not have to eat all of the fruit that is put in front of us. We can generate so much ourselves, and there is no need for a preoccupation with it. Love is a simple gift – you do not have to jealously guard it as it is there for everyone.

It is something that we believe mankind has forgotten; that matters have become too disseminated from the whole. You are like little islands. Like ants on a leaf trying to cross the river, and if one or two of you happen to be on the same leaf, it seems almost only by chance that you are able to paddle in the same direction. Such is the complexity of relationships and the unwillingness to accept the spirit that you are within, because there appears to be no motive or reward in direct consequence of this in the physical plane within the materialism that you live.

Happiness is such a key. You do not necessarily have to be with someone else in order to experience it, but it is important you are happy with who you are. That you are experiencing some sort of a change is fine. As long as you know you may head forward, and can see by way of your journey so far, that you are making progress within yourself. You can feel good about yourself and learn that the love you have for you is just a start. That there is so much more that can emanate from you towards others and towards all things.

The spirit within you is not a finite vessel that may withdraw at any time. You can entirely rely upon the flow and its content, so long as you think and wish to engage within the highest realm. The moment you have a lapse and you begin to feel a little twinge of guilt or negativity about yourself, you can generate those feelings within. So you overcome these dilemmas of life. Hopefully, you will find by doing this, you may fulfill further paths of your journey; seek and visually impact upon new and further glimpses of what life has to offer you.

You are all experiencing slightly different ways of progress, and all of the magic in the world cannot hold the reins for you. All of the materialism and all of the money cannot do it for you, for you have to do it for yourself. However, not that person you see in the mirror first thing in the morning … it is better to brush your teeth and wash your face, and then look in the mirror.

It is the same within. It is better to discover what you are on the inside so you may bring gifts to yourself; your happiness is the fundamental basic desire. It is not that all else fails to hit the mark, but that you can be much easier on yourself. You do not have to put yourself through all of that turmoil and grief, of wanting and needing, for love is always there – waiting to come and greet you.

At times we see love bedding
As a flower in our bed of life
A bud grows
It attracts our sense and willingness
To be a part of it

In all airs and breaths
In whatever walk we sit or stride
We all view love
As the greatest energy of all things

This may be love we view
This may be love we hold
But the greatest
Is that which we give to each other
Three fold ... again and again
To show we care

Clarity

We know from past experience do we not that the more we study something and seek clarification as to the various ins and outs of understanding, the more there seems to be to learn? It almost seems to grow before your eyes. An idea that was once thought small and trivial can blossom into something so magnificent and vast. You may be seeking the beginnings of an idea in one moment, and before you know where you are, you are writing a book.

Your perception of the world, what you see, sense, and think that exists is not what actually is. It is just a tip of a very big iceberg, a very large something else. It is not that you are small-minded, but merely that you are learning to use the magnifying glass you have in the correct manner, so you may be able to see slightly more. It does not have to be an object; it can be a sense within your mind, a reasoned thought. The more you study that particular thought, the more it seems to grow in front of you and you seek further clarification. The more you seek it, the wider your vision becomes, and your expanded mind can accept the knowledge and awareness of those things, which are around you. You can accept their concept of existence.

The more in-depth you think (or analytically, if you like) about a given situation or subject, the more you can bring out of that moment, then the more your understanding can grow within that moment. Your understanding grows, so next time you can recognize it and perhaps understand a little more. It is why no one person should ever think they know everything, for they do not.

Neither, is it a case of the blind leading the blind, for you are all able to perceive differences in various degrees. You can all move forward in one direction or another, you do not have to be led around like sheep in a field. You can all discover for yourselves, and that this is one of the primary purposes, the purpose to discover yourself.

You will receive greater clarity the more you study. Whether it is yourself, you are investigating, or whether it is the facet of somebody close to you or would wish to know. Is it not so, the more you engage with a new acquaintance on your journey, the more you begin to discover those little idiosyncrasies that go to make this particular individual? So it is with everything.

Thus, it is with spirit. The more you delve within, the more there is to find. This is why the seeking never stops. It is not that you become insatiable or out of control. You are not wanting more, but there is a quiet understanding that there *is* more to know. Then it will all be delivered upon its own time, as the story gently unfolds before you and you are able to grow with it.

The basis of all understanding is that you understand something; otherwise, you would not even be able to think. You are able to understand one thing and many other things follow. It is a natural process. You find that as other ideas and formulations are able to grow and take seed within your realm of understanding, other ideas germinate and flourish also. Something new – not regurgitated ancient text.

Yes, it is good to have a basis sometimes, to discover throughout history just where man has been, for there is so much knowledge to be gained from the past. But in order to do that it must be with an objective mind. For if you wish to make progress, you have to be here, now, where you are. In order to fully explore what your purpose is. It does not really matter what some ancient did long ago, so long as you do not try to emulate their action, for you do not know the circumstances.

Why would you wish to think so very deeply about someone else's existence, when you do not even have the control of your own? It seems that mankind is incapable of understanding the concept of the present and now. That locked in history is some idyllic formula that may be gleaned in order to save man's mortal soul from eternal damnation. But my friend, wait a minute – there is no problem. The only problem is with you – that you refuse to look. You refuse to discover for yourself the reality that exists in life.

Your present and your future are the most important aspects you have. With the momentum of life, you are able to move from moment to moment. To understand and to welcome each instant you have within your physical life span. If you just go with this momentum, you will then perceive so much more. Not only in your understanding of life, but life itself. Your physical life will appear to grow; it will seem longer to walk through the more you can fit into it. The more you open your life out the more you are able to perceive that you are growing within, and your time and space or your perception of it, seems to change also.

Now, this is not to say that you should go charging around the place trying to cram as many things into your life as possible. You could burn out. I am just merely trying to give you examples. That you may begin to understand how you may, if you wish, grow into something other than what you understand at this present time. The design of man is not a limited piece set on a drawing board. It is a limitless endless sky; there is no time boundary to your existence.

Know it my friend; there is no reason or excuse why you should not think and consider new ideas about yourself; new ways you may move forward and with courage. You may walk in amongst your landscape, and appreciate so much more. Everything can be fruitful, with no possibility of a negative influx coming within your life and causing ripples.

Positive thinking can balance the mind and crystallize the harmony within you and you are capable of harboring harmony, and capable of love far greater than you had ever imagined. You are able to sit and be at peace with yourself … of enjoying life in harmony with the aspect of God that we all are.

In time we walk
Our minds may not be clear
At times we struggle
Our vision in cloud

Memories can be as anchors
To our freedom
Yet when we look ahead
We can see the dawning of new time
Though physically
We may have none to give

And rain that falls from clouds that gather
And drums that sound a battle cry
Yet still we are beyond the gates
Yet still we are our view

With thought anew
How settled we can become
As crystal we bathe our soul
Our spirit bright

And clarity that makes us whole
Fresh and pure
In the light of all things
We are blest

Relationships

Your relationships with each other are based on many things, many facets and facts of your personality, and also the personality of the other person. It can be a long time before you meet anyone whom you feel understands you sufficiently to become a friend.

Friends can come along either singularly rarely, or in a gang of, like a row of buses. It could be that you make relationships with other people easily or with difficulty, and the difficulties you may have might not be of your making. They may not be of the other person's making either. It could be that you were from two different places so far removed that you could not strike any kind of relationship or bond.

This is strange is it not, because you would think: "Well, this is another fellow spirit traveler just like me, so why can I not bond with that person?"

Everyone has their own wish, their own pathway, and journey to make. All have to listen to the voice within them, whether they realize it or not – all do. Therefore, relationships that you form are not just based upon or inspired by an attraction, nor will you necessarily find in such relationships, something with which you can identify. Relationships that you form may be based on something entirely different. For example, you can regularly disagree with another, because you may have come from two completely different walks of life. Nevertheless, everyone you come into contact with will slightly alter your life, because you are forced to accept or reject his or her point of view.

I beg to say at this point, that some people on your side of life have a time when they refuse to change. When they refuse to search out new blades of grass.
"Oh no, I'm too old now, I can't change, I'm set in my ways."
How many times have you heard it? Yet, for many, it is like a cry of fear. Of being encased in the hard shell of the world that they have lived in. The hard memories of time passed. All that you are enduring now, they have all experienced. It is as if life has set hard like a crust about them. They cannot move; they will not change their way.

For some folk, it is best that you gently leave them to their wish, for they have said it or felt it, and meant it. Because they have found some sort of happiness or are satisfied. But for others, well, they only have to be shown a different seat on the bus – that they may look out of a bigger window upon their world. It may just be a phase of their life where they are up one minute and down the next, because their view of life has not stabilized. They are not aware of a certain formula or a given aspect of life that they find truthful or accept, so life is up and down.

The same could also be said for people who have found new concepts and ideas that work for them within a spiritual way. Their interaction with the material life throws them into direct conflict, and you can have a very similar seesaw life. This is difficult to resolve.

The relationships that you have are not just with each other; they are with everything, everything that is around you. When you establish relationships with all things, you can understand far more of the harmonic value of life. You may wish to have nothing at all to do with it and be blind or obstinate in your reasoning. On the other hand, you may try to understand both points of view and try to gain some understanding of an opposite of mind, for in that way you may see where they are coming from. Not to draw them to your way of thinking necessarily, but just to understand.

It is difficult I know, and some may say it is almost impossible, but what it will do for you, is it will increase your tolerance and awareness of others and how they think. Not just those who you already have some kind of closeness with, but with all those you do not see eye to eye, so that your relationship will bring you a little more understanding. You may gain a little more understanding about your own disadvantages, of your own lacks in communication maybe. You may become more at one with who you are and be kinder to yourself, but you do not have to be a martyr to your cause.

Simple to say, but not so easy to do. You must accept that not everyone is the same, and I know that many of you do understand this. It is also difficult to agree to differ when the opposite opinion fires so many emotions within you, for anger and resentment of that opinion can take a hold. The point at which that becomes a judgment upon that individual and second set of circumstances, is another area altogether, but for now, it is important you try to create a channel of understanding between you.

Explore another point of view; not in order to make it fit in with your view, but to discover your common ground, which is always to be the smoothest in life. Not every road is littered with precipices and sheer cliffs – there can be so much more to look forward to.

> We may all seek clarity in our vision
> Even though our mind may turn tricks
> It may even try to deceive the will of spirit
> To make right thought and action the way through
>
> We may give clarity the deed it deserves
> So that as clear water we may look to the other side
> To beyond the horizon that life produces
> And see it goes on and on in endless sway

Sleep and Your Astral Body

There are so many kernels of truth you may discover in your daily and bountiful journey upon your world. Perhaps we may turn for a moment, to those journeys you make when you are resting and asleep. Where you can travel boundless eons of time and space within a moment.

It is possible that some are even able to do this when awake or when in a meditative state. You may do this at your free will and engage with spirit at various times, so that they may impress you with ways in which you may proceed. Teaching you various aspects of learning to which you had not previously recognized.

These are likely to become clearer the more you sit for the development of your spirit within. You will gain in knowledge and understanding of those of the realms of spirit, such as from a higher existence.

There are many points in your life when you can interact with spirit freely, which does not have to be solely within the framework of meditatively sitting for spirit. It can happen at any time of peace and quiet and tranquility. That you may endeavor to greet your friends, those you have seen and maybe not remembered, and those you have not seen who are as old as time itself. For time is only a concept that belongs to your earth plane, it is not one of the real world as we see it. Time is not something that is on a plane of existence or exists with any existence. It is just a moment that is set – a division of space from one idea to another.

You abound on your journeys of light whilst in your dream state and you may wonder how these lessons can be incorporated into your daily life, when they are so oblique and difficult to interpret. How frustrating it is, when you wake up and you remember nothing. On the other hand, perhaps you do remember and manage to retain some of the information received or some of the journey you have made. That maybe you were going down some street or pathway you had never seen before.

It is not fantasy or an apparition of the mind. It is not some unseen force within or without that wishes to perceive control of each individual spirit traveler in sleep state. It is a genuine wish of your spirit to reach forwards, where you cannot ordinarily, in your physical form and reality. Such desire to progress is a part and direct function of your various bodies that go to make up your spirit and your physical body vehicle. There are many ways of traveling and there are many different realms within, where you may proceed. In fact, the numbers of realms are completely limitless. It is only the length to which you may allow yourself to proceed that is limiting.

At the beginning, it may seem strange and possibly frightening; however, it will never be hostile. You will never be put in any danger as such, but it is true to say that danger may be perceived, for whilst on the astral plane, the senses can be heightened considerably. Sensibilities of the mind can be affected by the fear and doubt you have inherited over the years. These are within your physical form. For they have driven and shaped all of these years up until this point in your life, and those fears and doubts can creep in from time to time and actually impinge upon the astral body as you travel. Do you see, that it can be possible to become frightened or upset at what you see or experience, because of the in-built fears you have been exposed to during your physical life on the earth plane?

This is not to say that the astral plane is a wasteland of vagabonds and suchlike, or that you should not experience it. It is useful to you, to establish the fact that you are able to see for yourself who and what you are – a vehicle in the physical form. Your body has no relation to you, the spirit, other than the fact that you are using it at present for the experience you are having. The astral or whatever aspect of your spirit, is not confined. Therefore, you can go about your business free and happy and not be tied to the mortal coil, as it were, so you are able to function on a more clear and level playing field of life.

You do not have to divide your time up into trying to calculate how you may dispel certain fears that have been with you for such a long time. For once you establish that you are indeed a spirit form, like we all are, then it is not just a perception, but reality – a fact. This very action should begin to quell those fears and doubts. Only, do not expect things to happen overnight, as these experiences have been heaped upon you over a long period, but all in good time.

You see, you can be good to yourself and just relax into it. You do not have to beat yourself with a hammer – a feather will do nicely. You can speak abundant words of wisdom if you wish, for it can just flow out from the spirit that you are. You are not a thing trapped inside a physical body. It is a very important part of your total journey here, to become relaxed in order that you can understand that your physical body is just another aspect of you, and not that you are an aspect of it.

Once you get the relationship right, as to who is doing what about your person, who is controlling what, you can allow your spirit within to shine out for the greater good and to a much larger extent. You not only perceive and conceive new ideas and new aspirations of thought that you had not previously experienced, but those thoughts may actually grow into sound truths. Not that you will just acquiesce to them, but hat you will treat them with respect.

You will find, because of your contact with who you are and have become, that you can go anywhere you wish, and not just necessarily within the physical body. For the physical body is only like cruising around on a bicycle and you maintain it, as it is your powerhouse that drives you. It enables you to get from one point to another, and it gives you the ability to communicate with the voice. However, you can engage your brain, the physical logistical machine, not only in the working of the physical body, but also in enabling new processes to filter onto the mind, concepts and ideas. Not all concepts and ideas are from spirit, some are the products of man-machine also.

We are not saying that everything is from spirit and that you are just a herd of animals with a spirit that happens to be unique. We are not suggesting that man the animal is set aside, just regarded as a lesser part of the whole and only useful as a vehicle for the spirit. Neither do we say, never mind about the body, for it is of no consequence!

Of course it matters, because although it is only of a temporary nature, it is a part of you, a part of your life and journey that you are having at this time. Every aspect of it:

including the pain, emotion, suffering, recollection and love; everything you experience as a human being on the earth.

Everything that has occurred is related and relayed to the mind, and is therefore accessible by the spirit that you are. This is how it all works. It is perfect really. You should not become complacent about your knowledge. You must use it for the benefit of all, so that everyone can gain. With the ever-flowing concept of even more to be given ... received through your spirit.

You are each far more
Than you think of yourself to be
Take courage
And fit into your shoes

Respecting Other People's Views

Each one of you could and should be more respectful to yourself. If you gave yourself some more respect, you may begin to regard yourself in a different light. In a more concerning light. How can you be respectful to others if you do not respect you? You have many problems on your side of life with those who give no one any respect, but they are not damned. No one is. They are just ignorant. They lack foresight and they are not in touch with anything, for they are untouched by their spirit.

Then how may we help these individuals? You cannot always go up to them and speak with them, as you could possibly finish up with a chair across your head. Therefore, it seems that the full frontal approach is inappropriate. As a society, you can introduce various laws in which you may try to curb their various activities, but at the end of the day, however much you try physically to restrain a mad dog, you still have to appeal to its better nature within. For it is only a symptom of its regressive spirit. It is only a reaction to a physical reaction that has been done to it. The same applies to those of you who are out of control, shall we say.

As we have said before, if it were not for the power of prayer you would all be at each other's throats, so there is much to be gained. And really, there are very many of you who actually do think alike, but one of the problems is that you are all isolated on islands. You all feel you are a lone voice.

What's more, do not think because of your knowledge and knowing (I will not say belief) that yours may be the only prayers that count. No, of course not. There is a vast multitude of those on your side who pray regularly for the same things, but perhaps coming from different fields or points of view. However strange their points of view may seem to you, they are all right within their way, and it is for no person to judge another by what he or she believes. It is not for us or anyone, to destroy another's faith. For it may mean the difference between that person at least trying to perceive a better self, than if they had not had that faith, and possibly, yet another one that you would have to find a secure room for! Do you see?

We would not wish to put anyone down. All of your fellow spirit travelers have the right to make their journey, whatever that may be. From time to time, we may describe follies they may make or discuss the religious doctrines they feel are right and just. Though, we only point these matters out so you in turn may know and see the truth for what it is. Through your knowing and your understanding, you will not just be able to perceive the truth, but know it in its entirety.

If a religion ostracizes all others for failing to make their faith their harbor – if they proclaim that theirs is the only way, then it is true to say they are misguided. For if, within your faith, you damn all others who do not follow you, you are truly misguided. Though, if you wish to damn others for their belligerence in following their knowing, that is different. It depends on what viewpoint you come from. For instance, if you happen to be an evangelist, you may well decide that those who walk the spirit path are all evil and condemned to hell. Not an ideal attitude and I am only using that as a point of reference. I am not poking fun at anyone you understand. It is just a case in point, if you wish. It is mankind's own folly to work out ideologies and theologies, which tie themselves in knots and so allows the truth to be misrepresented. If he takes this path then man will have to pay the price by not being able to perceive the difference between right and wrong. But those who tread the true path of spirit, the true path to upliftment of self, are to be applauded and encouraged.

So embrace everyone. Do not ask for their religious certificate. Just embrace them for who they are, for whom you see, for the spirit that is within – that they may shine out. It may be just a little glimpse, but it can come about. It can be so worthwhile to encourage and nurture the fruits of our labors, and may, over a long period of your life, come to give you gifts … gifts of love, of light, of patience and harmony with all.

Sometimes we listen to our thoughts
They may grace our table
They come in clusters
Or just as single entities

They can come in anger
Rising from the depths of self
They may bathe us in beauty
May leave us calm and be peaceful

Give birth to those thoughts
That are brave and strong
That give courage to your frame

Those thoughts who bring ill ease
Give them no energy
They will wither
Leaving the flower you are
To be bright in the field of life

Think a happy thought
Make greater purpose
Of each breath you take
Then give out the love you produce
As surely it will be needed
By someone someday

When Our Worlds Meet

As I have stated, every human being who makes the transition to our side, passes in the same manner at the moment of transition. It does not actually matter what is physiologically wrong with the body. That is irrelevant. The transition is but a moment, and the entire total of your life experience that is you, goes with you. Everything that has transpired within your lifetime on earth is accumulated and accompanies you. Every episode and feeling encountered. That is quite an amazing event ... all of those feelings of your whole life.

Another amazing event is the fact that we are able to equate and bring through information concerning the life once led upon your side of life, and this does require some practice. I will not say it is difficult for spirit to contact and break through into the physical world via mediums, but it does take some construction and instruction from those of mediumistic skills on our side of life as well. So there we have it, mediums on both sides.

At times, the communication, which is sought, is not particularly clear and not very accurate, and this can lead to some confusion. It can lead to some pointing fingers and claims of trickery. Some would even say that it is abusing someone at a time of misery and loss and is only a way of trying to attract attention to ones self. This is not so. For we, in the spirit realms, try to communicate with loved-ones that are still having their human experience, but we can have great difficulty sometimes, in securing any form of contact. Understand, inter-dimensional communication is always a great event on the spirit side of life, and we are so pleased that you continue to make contact at all.

Whenever there is a situation of public broadcast, of events between our worlds, the queues in spirit can be very long. For not only are there the relatives, friends, and past acquaintances of those travelers on your side of life who are attending the meeting, but also members of the public who would not necessarily be in that situation. There can be a veritable army. Plus, guides and helpers, various mediums, trainees and onlookers, and others who just happen to be there.

In regards to the way and manner in which we are doing now, well, it is at times like these that we can really shine out. It is so important that people can see we are not skeletons or shrouded misty figures walking in the dead of night. But that with patience, love, and trust from your side, we can be reanimated using the physical form that we just borrow for the time being.

It is so important that people can make themselves available for this kind of interaction. So that we may closer describe events and feelings, not necessarily of the past, not of the future, but of where you are now – in the present time.

We come to bring essences of ourselves
As we are fortunate to have this tryst
These seasons are worth
All the words that are written
And not for idle chat

These shared times of energy spent together
As vast armies that pull their worth in trains
Bringing what needs we must
Of positive will and focus
So they may be of use

For what good are words
Without thoughts behind them
Like empty dust that settles on the lampshade
Being whisked eerily around the airs of unseen
Instead of sparkling in the light

Materialism Will Hold You Back

There are so many earthly events you may discover upon your journey of light, intrinsically connecting you with the world of spirit. As things fall into place, and as your spiritual development unfolds, you receive greater wisdom and knowledge. You will recognize the power of love that spirit, the eternal creative life force is giving you. It is all freely given, and it will continue to flow so long as your work is diligent and caring.

The connection between man and his spirit; man that he is and spirit that he is, has long been established and fought for. In the past, man has tried to battle with it in order to control it. Even now, it is held by many that you call the shots, as it were. As you do, for you have the free will to pick and choose whether you acknowledge spirit or not. We, in the spirit light, would connect with everyone if we could and if they wished it, for there are so many more of us than there are of you, naturally.

It takes but a little time and a little effort on your part, to discover the many bounteous benefits that can be gained through just becoming aware of yourself. Never mind being aware of we, who are on our side. If mankind were truly aware, you would obviously not have the problems and trouble that you have now, which exist in your lives. It is only with your degree of awareness of self, of your spirit, that you may grow truly. There are many ways to weave a basket that will hold flowers, but there is only one way to weave a basket that will hold flour, so that it will not run out through the cracks.

You, for your part, must learn the art of control, for you think you can control everything. Not only your life and when you think it is a convenient time to stop it, but also, you feel that you can play with it for profit and gain, for business acumen. You claim the right above all others to produce life.

However, what you are producing, very clever though it is and sometimes a great blessing to many, is still within the physical. Perhaps you could say that the ordinary 'Joe' in the street is not the same. And yes, you are most probably right. Your average person, whatever that is, may break free from the constraints of your materialist environment. They may let go of that hold, so they can understand a little more. For that is the truth of it friends, materialism will hold you back. It will, in fact, keep you down and it will not give you joy. It will give you physical things in a physical world, but it will not and cannot ever give you love – for love is from within.

It would appear that human love seems to be difficult to acquire, contain, and make good use of, and the love of spirit, of God, is seemingly even more intrinsically trapped between layers you simply cannot reach. Just like having cellophane wrapped around an ice cream. You cannot eat it; you can never get to the ice cream. You can feel the cold through the cellophane, but find you cannot actually push

Materialism Will Hold You Back

your tongue through it and experience that energy, feeling your way through.

It is very similar to how spirit is, and how that contact with you is so important. You unwrap the ice cream first, layer by layer until you can see it. It is just a small gift, but it is so important. As with all gifts, they are of God – just as you are.

We must take time to reflect, and we must take time to unfold realization upon realization of truth. We must change the pages ourselves. We must strive for a higher understanding, for a greater awareness, and not be blind through the poisons and the quills of materialism.

The gifts you treasure
The ones that are not gifts
You do not need them

Your Choice

As you go about your daily life, you begin to access new paths to which you had not yet thought of. As you burrow your way through the undergrowth of your mind and learning processes, with the turn of every leaf you can begin to understand the relationships and ramifications upon turning each leaf. For is it not so, that as we are all linked in spirit, so we too all have a part to play in each other's destiny, in each other's learning and provision? We may all believe and think different thoughts, for the quest for free will has to be given, in order that truth may prevail through it.

Then why would we wish for one to go through life knowing a complete falsehood, or a load of rubbish, as you might say? Why could that be allowed – for one soul to become so misguided? The thoughts and feelings given to them being so misrepresentative of the truth.

There are several reasons for this. Firstly, of course, it is their choice. It must be left to every individual spirit to conquer the fears and doubts that are made manifest throughout their life, and overcome them. That is how you may ascertain a truth or an untruth, for an untruth has negative spots on it. It does not have the glow of truth, but a dull luster. It has a way of pinning one in ones' place, which inhibits freethinking and free will.

That you have choices is an expression of truth itself. There is your first truth ... that you have free will to decide for yourself. Thereupon, if you decide that the thoughts and wishes of what you perceive God to be, places restraints upon the mind and will of man as is expressed in many outdated and outmoded ideas and doctrines, then that is the expression that you wish to take. And we, as free spirit, although we may acknowledge it, it does not mean that we sanction it. It just means that the knowing is there – that we are aware.

We are not trying to be subtle and mysterious about how a belief is structured, about how free truth really is, but just to say that we cannot make a judgment upon others' lives. What we try to do when we communicate with you is to make observations, in order to open up opportunities for debate and learning. You may then make up your own mind as you wish.

This is the way and manner in which we suggest that you try to communicate with spirit, so things are out in the open. Then you can all see.

Not to say: "This is the right path, this is the one to take, all the rest of it is nonsense!" "You must follow what I believe, for I know better than you!"

That is being dictatorial. How can you say that you give free will to others if you then take it away?

Well, that in itself is only a matter of opinion is it not? So we see many sides, like a coin, which is not just a flat piece of metal, it has many sides to it. There are always questions and answers concerning all facets of learning, of life, of truth and inner knowing. It is built up layer upon layer, as levels of understanding increase.

If your side of life and our side of life did not have communications with each other, then we too would not move forward, therefore, it is to our mutual benefits that we do. Once views are aired then we can all understand a little further within the, not discrepancies, but the individualities of truth. How truth may be perceived and understood for everyone's benefit.

There are many maligned ideas as to how progress should really be made, and how that progress may be thrust upon others. However, progress is all up to the individual. You cannot push a worm through a hole in the fence … it will always turn its head one way or another!

Interpretation is Everything

At times, do you think that maybe you are limiting your self-expression; your expression of the spirit that you are, by trying to conform to some pre-conceptual ideas as to the mark you may wish to achieve? Is it not correct that you have a certain set of goalposts you feel you have to climb, in order that you may reach some expectation, or a mark of respect? Somehow, you have to attain this position before others can regard you as an accomplished voice within a given area.

It would seem to us that from a small being of light inhabiting your human form, that not only do you move through your journey of self-determination on the one hand, but that you have this other kind of criteria, which is laid out before you. In other words, you have to attune yourself to a certain set of landmarks upon your journey through the world on which you live. It is as though you have to walk along a pathway lit by these landmarks, and that you have to pass them in the correct manner prescribed, in order to receive merit, in order to receive a justification for your journey.

The problem is that these merits and markers are also in fact, quite limiting to your overall understanding of life's intricacies. So instead of learning the benefits of expanding ones awareness of oneself in the truest sense, you are only subscribing to some illicit viewpoint. You feel you have to receive certain documents, evidence if you like, as to your worthiness or not.

Let us say you have worked hard in a given area, you are now qualified to practice this expertise to both benefit others, and yourself, and you have all of this information and the documents as evidence to prove this. I venture to say however, that in doing so there are many other aspects of your life, which may have been left on the sidelines. I know you are living a material life, and need to climb upon the material ladder in order for you to gain both self-respect and knowledge and reliance upon oneself, for in truth you have no one else. But, having done this, are you also aware by this dual process of learning, which you have undertaken and accomplished, that you are also at the same time, potentially placing boundaries before you?

Yes, you benefit from the glory of the knowledge you have received in respect of the given frame of reference. However, at the same time, instead of limiting yourself to a specific understanding, you could have become aware of much greater intricacies and greater understandings, thus enabling you to move further along the learning curve.

I am saying this to try to put across that sometimes in life, we feel we have accomplished something, when the real fact of it is, we have actually accomplished very little. This could be said of the various doctors, politicians, and scientists, who may be of an authority in certain areas, but who lack the ability to delve beyond their narrow scope of understanding. They may lack the ability to express their inner feelings to others, because they are out of touch with these emotions – a bit like skimming the surface.

The process of your learning should not be restricted to one place or point of view, and you cannot say that a specific area of science is that specific anyway, for it will overlap many other areas of science, thought, technology, and advancement. If you have the courage to go on, the process of learning is limitless.

However, in advancement of your knowledge of spirit and matters concerning your own inner development, the way in which you could become a more agreeable human being, involves a process of learning far greater than any of these aspects we have so listed. The process of learning is indeed far more engaging, for each posed question, each statement of fact, each thoughtful answer requires so many more questions and answers, and yet again more questions and answers. It is then that we begin to discover just how limitless the voice of truth can actually become.

You could say it is a little similar to plowing a field. If you plow it just once a year, then between the times of plowing the weeds will only come back growing just as prolifically as before, and spread their seed everywhere. The more detail you put in – perhaps, the more you plow to disturb those sometimes-cursed plants, the more you may see other things that can become yielded and enlightened from the soil. You may uncover other riches other than just weeds.

So it is with unfoldment, that through diligence and involved understanding, the cycle gradually becomes clearer as to the nature and process of learning via your spirit.

You cannot say at any one point: "I have succeeded," given that we should all be aware that the process of spirit teaching and learning is ever evolving, is ever growing as you grow. As you push forward your otherwise limited concept to further enlargements upon your understanding, the further you can obviously see. Then the more you see the more you realize there is so much more to see, for not every stage of your unfoldment may appear to contain the same amount of heightened awareness.

You might think: "Oh, that was a bit of a let down; I thought it was going to be this, and it was not."
Yet, unperceived by your self-awareness, you have actually shifted and understood something else you had not realized was there ... and so the journey goes on.
It is not that you arrived at point 'A' and found the piece of paper you should have collected was in fact given to someone else or maybe not there at all. It was not that you necessarily arrived at the specific point you had already perceived in your mind. It is that you arrived at the point you were meant to arrive at, and it did not actually involve a piece of paper at all!

Do you see what I am saying? That you may have preconceived ideas about yourself, you may have ideas that you wish to reach point A instead of point B. Perhaps you did not know point B existed, but by taking the journey, you may have actually discovered point B. Such a vantage point will then let you see point A in a different light. You may discover that by putting limits on your expectations, the journey teaches you little other than perhaps that you have passed another post. The post may be meaningless; it may be full of woodworm and good for nothing other than burning or discarding altogether.

It can be a minefield that we walk, searching for the signposts of life when all along they are there. It is just dependent upon your idea of what you expect. It is just that sometimes you have to be taken to a different viewpoint in order to discover where you are within your plan, within your relationship to everything seen and unseen. Then you can perceive another new horizon panning out in front of you.

Speak not of lies
Give not one thought an airing
It closes the eyes to truth
And casts doubt
Upon the experience
You are to make
In the purpose of your journey

Speak only of truth
And if a lie comes upon your mind
Do not let it out
Make it sink into oblivion
From whence it has come

You Are
Your Own Angel

One of the observations, which is so fascinating when in the journey of the physical life, is that it would appear that there are so many things working against the spirit within you from being heard. You are carried along just as leaves on a stream being taken to the ocean; and perhaps you may in observation from time to time, think how lucky you are for being the leaf floating on the water. However, without any direct effort involved within, to enable you to paddle to the side of the stream and to observe the whole matter from a different perspective, if you are not capable of allowing yourself those spells within a dimension within, then how can you come to terms with the grief or with the suddenness of your passing? Or, with any other passing of any other fellow spirit traveler who happens to be close, or shared your path, however briefly.

It just seems to be blind acceptance that death is the very inevitable outcome that life produces, the concept of just maintaining equilibrium of mass, which you feed and water from time to time, until it eventually gives out. You maintain all efforts to continue life at whatever the cost, for it is so precious and death so final. And yes, life is precious, but then no more thought is given to what actually occurs.

This perfection that you seek is not an unreality; it is not a ghost of a thought or a dream that just dissipates with time. Neither is it just involved within the malfunctioning of the mind, brought on by some bereavement or a wish for eternal life. It is none of these and it is for your sake, it is real, pure, and abundant.

It would appear that man chooses not to wake up to the reality of the beast that is within his mind – that beast called death. The beast that man tries to conquer, overpower or prolong in some hideous way, by maintenance of pain, and very often exhausting the physical frame in the process.

In addition, I have to say a process, which perhaps should have been curtailed long ago; with each human valued beyond all coincidence of reality. Maybe then, you would finally feel you have the control upon life that you seek; that you can finally push the right buttons and call yourselves God, for it would seem you feel you have the power in the physical world to create anything!

However, the spirit has a far greater power than this. The spirit within, once it is acknowledged and ignited, is not like a firework that springs through the night sky and disappears. It will gather momentum and become stronger and brighter on your journey that is forever.

Do you see what I am getting at?

You go to your cemeteries and mourn, and yes, why should you not mourn the passing of a loved-one so dear? We would not decry that fact, but there are so many other emotions that you can feel within you at the time of the passing of a loved-one, other than mourning the event and your own private loss. It is a sad fact that this should be so devastatingly traumatic.

In truth, whether it is your relations, friends, or mere acquaintances, at the time of their transition, the overriding feeling should be that of acceptance and happiness. Of being at one. That another traveler has not succumbed to some ill, but has traversed to another level of existence, to a moment beyond yours, and can be closer than that in an instant. It is the transition of thought, of purer and higher fulfillment. A transition from your side to our side ... and is to every spirit, home.

The majority of you only have a specific containment within the mind as to what life and the prospect of it is. You may say with boring repetitiveness that no one has ever come back from being dead. Well, that of course, is a complete and utter untruth. You could even say that many of you come to our side on a very regular basis, are forever popping in and out in one form or another. It does not matter whether your physical appearance has actually passed from your physical realm or not. It is the fact that you have made the journey and you have been aware of the observations you have made. You have brought back tangible evidence that you have been somewhere, not within the mind – but without the body. That you have actually manifested upon your intrinsic being, that you have made a journey from A to B and come back again.

With that thought in mind, you cannot be anything but lifted by it; it speaks volumes, and these journeys may increase your understanding and awareness of the true facts. You know it for a sure fact, for you go there often and see for yourselves.

Friends, do not weep when you stand at the graveside watching a box descend into the ground or going within a fire, it is not necessary. You may take great comfort and joy from all of the times that you yourself exist within the spirit light, within all of those journeys and magnificent aspects that you visit on a regular basis.

They should not cause you concern for they are just different aspects of the same voyage that we all make. All of us, in all realms, make journeys my friends. It is natural, a willing glimpse of who exactly you are. It is a little like looking in the mirror and finding out there are more warts than you had realized. Or perhaps discovering pores within your skin that you had not previously seen. Is your hair going grey? Maybe it is and you had only just noticed, but others had noticed long ago.

It is down to your perception of who you are. If you wish to look in the mirror and see just what you want to see, then that is what you will see. You may not notice the grey hair for many years, but it is still there. And it is the same with the way and manner in which you conduct your life and in how you seek to find your higher self, or to even recognize it may exist. It is but a step, a single landmark within your horizon of many landmarks that you will come across. Once you have gained the trust and knowledge of the idea, of the concept, then you can proceed.

You may decide that one particular statue or other is your harbor, is your angel of mercy, but the angel of mercy that possesses you, is you. You are your own angel. You are your own savior, and you are your own path to be pulled from darkness, to be graced by the light of infinite wisdom and love.

You are part of all there is and all there is yet to be. Every single breath you take now and every mind frame of your life that you possess within your spirit being, is the basis of countless journeys that you may make within the realms of spirit. All is bountiful, be not afraid. What you perceive as justice is not as justice is. The real truth of exactly what your happy make-up is, of your design of the aspect of God that you are, should always be and remain your destiny.

There are those we suspect in high repose
They are glossy and painted
They sing and play as no earthly giant
Yet beyond the eye exists the angel within us all

Beyond the realm of physical life
The light of stars the spirit bright
We are all the angel of our desires
We are all as great and perfect souls

We cannot see blinded by our own lack of vision
Of angels, we are every one
Perfection we are and must strive with every breath
We ask each other to be our guide and there we rest

Ghosts

There are some entities, which are not really spirit at all – ghosts. They are attached to fabrics of material life, and they can be the result of a traumatic event or just be an essence of the spirit that has been left behind at a certain place. They do not pose any harm because they are not entities within themselves. They are like a photographic negative that has been left on. They can illume themselves now and then, using, and in conjunction with, the energy of the spirits of you on your side of life passing by, just by your presence. Not forgetting of course that you are 98% water and other gases and carbons, which are combined at this particular time.

Your influences, along with your spirit or the way you are thinking, can also have an impact upon that focus of energy. In addition, I must say here, that I am not saying that only people with maladjusted minds will see such events. I am merely saying it can be available just to certain people who think in a certain way, and only those see it. It is a repetitive movement or image, which will appear similar or the same in its activity, regardless of the events taking place around it. They are static images and would not be able to react to you – a bit like pressing the re-play button.

It is a strange occurrence, but nonetheless, a fact of life. What you would term as a ghost, is in fact, a ghost image. This imprint may come and go, but is not real in any sense, material, or spirit. They may appear to walk, glide, or drift, and, of course, as we know, this can be in open countryside, on a road or wherever. Whatever happened at the time has just left its mark upon the landscape, like a scar, a scar that has healed. Therefore, we are of the conclusion that as it is a scar that has healed, the spirit who left it has moved forward from that moment in time.

It is also a possibility that buildings will have these moments. As a sensitive, you may walk into a room of a house for example, and momentarily see it for exactly the way it was when originally built, with all of the love and care and craftsmanship that went into its construction. By exactly the same stroke, in a split second the whole fabric of this building you were observing, changes back into how it is now.

It is interesting that it can happen both with those who were of the spirit on the physical plane, and also to some inanimate object like a building, but true nevertheless.

There are ancient monuments and artifacts that hold so much vital information, and not just from their type or design structure, but also in what you might pick up from them when you walk close by to one. Or maybe when you pick up an object, the psychometry of it; it emanates a physical and spiritual power of its history.

It is quite unrealistic perhaps to think that in man's endeavors to become closer to God he erects edifices, when the truth of it is that God is within all of us. Yet, there has been so much feeling; tenderness, harmony, and yes, love there, even though it has been abused over many centuries;

all of those buildings contain these emotions and it is why they are so attractive. Take the love and the harmony out of a building and you are just left with bricks and mortar ... molecules really, and not a lot else. It is not just a history of what went on and why it became a relic. It is the very fact of its standing through so many generations. Of all those who have been around it and even clambered over it trying to mend it, or whatever.

These structures are, and can be in a perfect spot of course, designed for very specific functions of which you now know little, as with those of the Incan Empire, or the Pyramids, or Stonehenge. When you find a roadway that was perhaps designed and built thousands of years ago, it can bring a certain spiritual harmony to your being as you see it or stand on it. This is not a physical emotion response to what you see, but the spirit entropy, which is within it. Because so many thousands have stood as you now stand – their memory may be linked with you.

Therefore, you see how these things may affect your spirit. May affect you and enlighten your mind, the spirit that you are. It may be just a load of bricks going into the distance ... but it has a feeling. It is most important, as you become more aware and more developed in the spirit way that you are able to pick up senses and feelings. Not just from the people you meet, but from the rooms you enter, feeling harmony or disharmony from places that you go.

You may see many wonders in your life and all have their internal input to give you. They all have their print, their photographic image of just who and what passed by them, whether in fear or joy.

We may show love
We may bring it to the surface
As it bubbles and ferments its way
From the spirit deep within us
From the very heart of soul
To become the effigy of our reason

The staff of our standing
We may then lay at the feet
Of those who have none
Who have lost their way
And have forgotten
What real love feels like

Poltergeist

There are those on our side of life who, shall we say, lived a less than provident life, and may have had a certain unhealthy attitude of mind. They did not wish to progress whilst on earth and still do not on our side, and will remain so until they wish to change their mind. These people may come back to dwell half between the spirit light and the physical world. They may bring large amounts of negative energy with them, and you might be able to sense and feel those vibrations of deistic matter.

They are spirits, just like you and I, but maybe wish only negativity. They have not even grown to the first post as they are immersed in negative vibration. You call it poltergeist activity, and it can be quite disturbing on your side of life when you do not have things moving in harmony.

We must say here, that this is a rare situation and it is not to be confused with the physical phenomena circle. Wherein, this is an arrangement, and it is begun with an opening prayer or invocation of love and protection from one side to the other. The physical contact made here is one of harmony, and brings much needed communication to the physical world in which you live. It is driven only by the exchange of love between our two worlds.

In contrast, these former manifestations may make themselves apparent at will, causing a disturbance and just generally making a wretched nuisance of themselves with their unwanted activities and presence. They can also attach themselves to people or to places; to the fabric of buildings, houses, or even parts of the countryside, and may even be seen occasionally. Some of them may be souls who are trapped, as they have not found the light, but there are others, who have actually refused the help by those on our side.

There is some work in this area that mediums on your side of life are able to do. In showing them how they may be released from their entrapment. You may be better equipped to help in some circumstances, being on your side, because they do not want to leave the physical plane. They have just one yearning, to be with you, to be where you are. They do not wish to leave the physical side of life and do not see the benefit or the possibility of return in love to further their progress as spirit. Even though we show them love and purity they sometimes do not accept it, for they do not understand. No matter how much persuading we do, with all the love and best intentions, they will not move.

They may take us on the guise of being demons, as it may have been a view that they held whilst having their physical journey. It depends so much upon the human consciousness at the time of transition to our side of life. You see, history teaches us we must take on the challenges our ancestors have left us, regardless of what they are, and this holds the same for these spirit entities. Therefore, if one passes and remains unhappy, remains in the low form of which they have attained, they sometimes need help in bringing themselves forward so that progression may be made. That they may take their rightful journey instead of dwelling in the past.

Now, it is possible that you may be rather unfortunate and have attracted these negative sources, and instead of interacting with spirit from the higher realms and making your life dream possible, these lower entities can make it turn sour and may spread fear.

"Doctor, I have voices in my head, please take them away!"

Unfortunately, for some of you the voices will be the wrong ones and it can be catastrophic to your life, and it may need careful analysis with a wary and knowing expert. This may not necessarily be something to be treated with drugs my friends. If you are infested (as it were) with a disturbed spirit, you have to call upon the powers of light and love. Of we, of the spirit light – to guide and keep you safe and to have these extradited as quickly as possible.

You see, not all communication from spirit is of the positive manner and there can be times when you could be interrupted by the negative forces. For although, we, of the spirit light, try to keep them inter-reactive within our side of life, sometimes they break free and move between planes, being mischievous. They can become solitary, seeking out those of the weak or disturbed mind whom they may then infiltrate.

It is very important that should an individual be afflicted with such a negative vibration, that they do not and must not feel they have to deal with it on their own. They must enlist the help of one of mediumistic skills from your side of life, who will then be able to facilitate a greater involvement of their energy in order to resolve the situation.

This is not the stuff of nightmares my friends. It is just a fact of life. These spirit entities, unhappy persons as they are, do exist, and have not accepted the fact perhaps that they have to atone for their past wrongs. Instead, they are bent on continually causing mischief and mayhem.

Now, once again, I know that somebody reading this book may be feeling fearful and frightened, and thinking: "How do I know if the things that are happening around me are of good or bad intent?"

Well, do they give you an understanding of love and truth? Do you sense peace and harmony, thoughtfulness, compassion and grace?

We, of the higher realms, are very bright and may shimmer and sparkle, and of course, everything we bring is with the highest of love. We suggest that you also remain in this way, but that if you do become engulfed by some tragic circumstances, you may always ask for protection of the highest. If you seek help as we have described, all will be well.

The real world exists for you to explore, every facet of it – all of its encompassing and varied nature. Caress the joys of each other, experience through knowledge and truth, and all can be joy. There is no casting out. All is given, received, and blessed within our walks, for we are all spirit. We are all within the realms of light ... we only have to realize the truth.

If love exists
Where it lives
There can be no negative will
If negativity rears its head
It must be that the owner
Has forgotten what love feels like

This then must be a sad day
A moment lost
Unlike that which reveals
How without love
We may be so desolate
And empty

Do Not Be An Island

It is a fact, that if each of you were an island, your view of the world would be utterly different to what it is now. If you did not interact with others around you, how would you really feel? How could you presume to take on any mantle of success or failure, or observe anything other than with your own eyes? You may think you would perceive a clearer picture. But would you really? You could then go on and make a mistake perhaps, as to the perception of what and who you are and what there is that lies before you. Without someone else's opinion, is it not true that you could actually have misjudged something? You could have utterly misplaced the point of what you see, of what your encounter is.

So it is with life friends. For when you come upon a fellow spirit traveler blinded by ignorance, encased within solitude and never looking outside, how might that person actually perceive anything else other than what they want to see? How can we open their eyes? It is difficult is it not, to ignite a flame of such a damp fire?

Although, it could also be an observation that if this fellow spirit traveler has been solitary and not felt the need to communicate, that they may be right, and we are wrong? It might be the case that their own thoughts are clean and pure, with no possibility of contamination from the outside world. That in actual fact, what they see is truth, for it is untainted by anything other than with their own eye.

Well, yes friends, I suppose you could say that, it is an easy way out, but without the interaction, how do you learn to give love? How may you then seek to move within the forest if you are blinded by ignorance? Will you make mistakes; will you stumble and crash into branches of those trees that have fallen? You will not know the terrain, you will not know where the forest ends, and the cliff begins.

We cannot be blinded by our thoughts of the past. I know they help to color and shape our lives, but when you see the mistakes for what they are, you have to be able to do it from the right perspective. If you do not, you do not see the full learning curve you have been given, and the only manner in which you may do that is to move away from it, so seeing it in its true light.

There are so very many problems you could face and encounter, and not just problems of a minor nature. Indeed not, things of great harm and disturbance can beguile your lives, lulling you into a sense of fear, depression, and doubt – it is everywhere. You may lift yourselves and each other from this insanity, but it might take time, for slowly can move the wheels of the industrial mind. Adjustment takes time on your side of life. You cannot build a factory in the middle of a forest glade and expect there to be no objection, not least of all from the wildlife that lives there.

Overall, you do have your own picture to paint. You have been given your blank canvas and the brushes, but it is up to you to mix your own colors, to find natural harmonies and balances. You may create your own meaning, with your own hues; so your picture is, and becomes an individual expression of the eternal spirit that you are. Not necessarily an expression that is admired by others, but one recognized as being different. Familiar, yet unfamiliar – new, and yet you have somehow seen it before.

Whatever you are feeling, try to peel back the zips on your eyes. Rub them; throw water on them, whatever you have to do to open them up.

This is not a secret society friend; this needs to be walked together. We are not intrinsically enemies of each other it should not be so. We are all brothers and sisters of the same light, the same truths, and the same difference. We do not wish you all to be the same, and neither do we wish you to be an island of barrenness, empty and devoid of all vegetation. For with such, the tides can quite easily overcome you, those tides of humanity can swamp you out and drown your colors and your vibrancy.

I have my view and I will not part with it
Not one iota will I leave
My lips are sealed my mind is closed
How can I see - how can I hear thee

We are but the ship we feel we sail
Do not leave your deck for another boat
Do not leave your mind for another
Make good what you are
Sail into the distant light
Be calm upon the ocean of life

Be not an island
But sail into the arms of others
Your foot ashore
The sails of your mind as bright illuminations
Of words and meaning
Not trussed up but flying open and free

You are not an island my friend
But as perfect as every grain of sand that laps its shore
And every grain may join with many others
And become long stretches of gold as the summer sun

Be not an island
Be free
Let the wind of thought take you

Just
A Little Observation

As you cling desperately to the direction you feel your lives should strive to take, we observe that sometimes you break off more than you can chew. You preciously hold a certain part of your life plan in the palm of your hand, and sometimes what can happen, is that you try to break off the section, which you feel does not fit into it. However, instead of just breaking off the piece that you felt did not qualify, you can break off a much larger piece, and now find that it is completely different to what you had imagined it to be.

I will try to put it another way. You may feel quite contented with a certain aspect of your life, and yet other aspects may not seem quite so fruitful. Therefore, you try to improve them, to make them fit the mode and model you have set, for how you feel it would please you to be. So then, you try to manipulate certain areas of that aspect of your life, and sometimes you can try too hard and it distorts the picture, and you can be left with a completely different scenario. You also find that you then get adverse reactions from other people.

This is one of the situations you may find difficulty with from time to time, with feeling that you are out of control of your life plan. That you have gone too far and wish to take steps backward along the path, and undo the parts you wished to improve upon. Because sometimes, your view of improvement is not other people's perception of it, if you took the idea that it was necessary to involve these people in your life in the first place.

Consequently, it would appear that life is, and can be, so complicated by these factors. That Jill cannot always please Jack all of the time, but that sometimes Jill must stand and other times Jack must stand, and sometimes the two must just beg to differ. There are certain characteristics of every one of us that we do not find wholly agreeable, but we usually find that we can still accept a fellow spirit traveler nonetheless, because of all of the other aspects that we are so akin with.

Our observance is that some people have such great difficulties in not only recognizing they may have broken off a bit too much and misshapen their character, but also have problems in retrieving themselves from situations. That because they jumped in with both feet they feel they must drown, perhaps in spite of and despite the situation being improved by other sources, because of loss of face. It is that old stubbornness of human nature I suppose. That some people just cannot bend, no matter how hard you try to reason with them. They will not see the errors they make and then end up all bent and twisted within the mind and thought processes.

Just A Little Observation

These are all the things you have to take into account with people. We recognize that you and your fellows are not infallible. None of us are. We all have desire to learn and to grow within our characters. We all wish for change, for it would become a dull life would it not, if it were not for improvement and moving forwards?

So, perhaps when you feel you have not attained the right result, or fear you are not going in the right direction within your life as you would hope, do not try to change too much in one go. You may break off a bigger piece than you had thought and it may be you do not have the right glue to stick it back in place, or that the right glue you require is very expensive and costly to your learning processes. Just be patient and gentle with yourselves.

Do not misunderstand me. I do not mean you should just sit there and accept whatever life has to throw at you. No, for life requires active participation, it requires energy, compassion, fulfillment, and so many other things besides.

Effort

Effort. Sometimes, you make so much of it that it is almost as if you manufacture it larger than life, and in order to surmount the smallest hurdle. Occasionally, it may seem that although you do it for the best intentions, that it can somehow either be led astray or just be completely insufficient for the object of your desire. Yet, it might be that despite all your efforts, what you desire is not available to you. And you will notice I did not say impossible – for nothing is impossible.

You see you must never think you have failed or that you are a failure. It is just that the availability of a particular understanding or a point of life is presently unavailable to you. You will acquire higher modes of understanding, of knowledge and wisdom throughout your life, except it will become available through your discerning eye, through the wisdom and knowledge that you gain. There is not any real advancement without wisdom, without it being available to you, so that you may breathe it and be it.

Knowledge and wisdom is not to be plucked from the ether and it is there all of the time, every moment of your existence. Not just within the physical realm you are in, but of all existence. It is there for you to access, it is for you to be receptive and bring yourself to the place where you may receive and learn, so that more can be gained.

At times, all of this effort may seem wasted. It may appear to you that you are making no progress whatsoever. I believe all of us sometimes feel we are making little or no progress or headway in our lives; that we hope and pray for God's involvement so we may glean a little more. That we may understand we are on the right path after all and not in another cul-de-sac, but the path of our unfoldment.

Yes, life is a serious business, but we must all have laughs and jokes and play the fool at times, for it is so necessary that we feel and embrace all aspects of ourselves. It is within the embracing, that you will find in situations no matter how painful, that your knowledge, learning and unfoldment, may stand and prepare you for greater and greater tasks ahead.

Each movement that you make is further testament to your will to learn, by gaining and accessing the answers. However, it is not to be achieved by falling over each other or pushing each other out of the way in a bid to be ahead of the next person, by trying to gain knowledge more quickly than anyone else. Nor by putting others down for having attained what you have not. You all have access to the same water trough; you do not have to squeeze anybody out.

In addition, the choices you make are not necessarily those that you have to stick with for the rest of your entire journey, for your feelings may change.

You may move within different circles. You may gain a desire to improve yourself through other windows of opportunity. You may take other learning curves and invite other understandings to be illuminated before you. You can always take on board that which you would wish to fulfill your life and your heart, just so long as the intention is that of a higher understanding and learning.

Agreement is not blind, agreement is not sleepless, it does not wish for compromise. Agreement is knowing and understanding a matter. Knowing it and understanding it, so that you are looking at it from the same point as the inquirer – as the letter of the agreement states. All aspects of life are very similar. All are for growth, learning, and understanding, and you may wish to agree to certain parts or not. You may take on board various feelings; those that have been supplied by others that you feel touch parts of you, so you feel a shared learning.

This situation in particular is seldom felt, but it is nevertheless a constantly available emotion. It tends to be when there are specific disasters or actions that touch the hearts of many. You feel a common bond – and it suddenly leaps up in your throat. Is it not amazing that so many could produce the same thoughts and feelings of closeness, of an affinity with each other?

Well, that common bond is how you may feel all of the time if you so wished, but unfortunately, it is because mankind has isolated themselves from each other that they do not feel this so often.

You may gain what you wish to take at any time from the actions in which you are involved with, for the growth of your learning, and the tools you need for growth are all available to you. Although you may make plans that you will move within a certain direction, in a certain way, you know it very often does not come out like that. You may sit there and scratch your head, wondering why you bothered making plans in the first place, because they never seem to turn out the way you expect.

In fact, the circumstances, which have been given to you to learn and take on board, have perhaps been for the better, or to do with a different mode of understanding and comprehension. It is always possible for you to gain more, but life as we know it is not only for you own personal gain.

Gain is interesting and necessary for you to help and understand yourself, to understand in a much more relaxed and better manner those things you need to know.

All is there before you, and one of the most important things you will discover is that you may give love and understanding back. You may give all of that stimulation you receive back to others, so that they too may climb those pleasant hills. So they too may see the wondrous flowers upon their journey ... that they too may understand their true nature and birthright.

> The more effort you make
> The broader the casting of the net
> The greater abundance of choice
> May be laid at your table
>
> It shows you the difference
> Of idea and vantage you may gain
> Whilst reflecting
> The positive cause you have given
> Upon the instance of your journey
>
> Do not waste the boundaries of your effort
> For lesser strains
> Give them the greatest cause
> For growth and promise
> You will be rewarded

The Importance of Forgiveness

It is so hard for many on our side of life to come to terms with or to forgive themselves for wrong doings done by them. They wish to express how important forgiveness is, as well as needing to be forgiven by the recipient of their actions and all of those who are in line of the knock-on effect. If forgiveness cannot come from those whose lives have been affected by their actions or thoughts, then it can then be so difficult for them to deal with their remorse.

There are so many in the spirit world who wish to be able to communicate once again to your side of life. I do not believe it is possible for you to appreciate just how much sorrow there can be if there is no forgiveness. It becomes such a hurdle to overcome, for this in itself may trap the machinery of being able to once again feel that there is any point. Yes, even those on the spirit side of life have these feelings, regardless of their significant understanding of where they are. Even regardless of that, they can still be trapped within the moment of negative impulse.

I would have to say; to a degree, their actions have rebounded on them, had a karmic effect if you like, upon their spirit and their wholeness. That they may not traverse this indiscretion or abandoned morality – that there is seemingly no path to which they may elude the ravages of an unforgiving soul. Nevertheless, those who are within this entrapment do seek from time to time to communicate with your side, to try to relieve their agonies and experience some way of opening a new door.

Now, it has to be said, that even despite the many attempts by those on our side to accommodate these spirit travelers within their complex situation, bringing comfort and solace sometimes seems inadequate. Some are simply inconsolable in their grief, of the destruction they have wrought, and you who are on the earth are able to help them in this way. You are able to give them just a little light or a little thought in their direction. They feel far more benefit because it is coming from the physical side of life.

This is not necessarily from a reality point of view, you understand. It is just a part of the entrapment that is within them, in which they find themselves. If they could only allow we, on our side, to truly help them, they would most probably recover far quicker. However, the act of being able to communicate with those loved ones they have left on your side of life and to ask and receive forgiveness in a direct manner, is of far greater importance on occasions. It seems that for some, nothing else will do. This may help you to be able to understand the depths to which forgiveness is so necessary for the progress of the spirit.

For example, you have to learn to forgive yourselves, for your own transgressions or misdemeanors upon life's rich pathway. We all have them – little skeletons in the closet! We all have things in the top drawer that we would rather forget, and occasionally, you will find they just pop out of their own volition.

You may think: "Oh my word, what on earth is that doing there. I put that away long ago, and here it is looking up at me?"

Amusing now maybe, but at the time of recollection it brings hot flushes to the face. Yet, in that recollection, you are able to perceive and even perhaps gloat over just how far you have come from there, from that moment in time. It is just sewn on to the tapestry of your memory. With loving thoughts, you may even perceive some of those effects upon your life with kindness, for without them you would not be where you are now.

"What, did I really have to do all that mischief in that public house or bar (or whatever it was) in order for me to be here now?"

In a way you did, for all of your actions throughout your life have in fact brought you to this place, where you have gained new expression. You have gained new insights and knowledge within the truth of life, and without them, you would still possibly be making similar judgments about events that happened only last week, instead of many years ago.

For that reason, it must follow that with the continued developments of your spiritual nature, through your ever-searching and longing mind for the truth, that you have made many leaps forward within your lifetime. This means that somewhere along the line, you must have done some good deeds too, in order to enjoy this present repast. It is a joy you have earned. You have arisen to the challenges set before you, of exploring and indulging yourself upon the search for truth, along the path of love.

Having forgiveness for all of those past indiscretions does not mean to say that they have completely gone away, but at least you can feel more at peace with them. So long as they do not come out too often. It is a reminder only of where you have been, and it is in the past that they need to remain – and you can only acknowledge their defeat to the past.

You are bridled to the path you are now experiencing and you will find greater strength and greater honesty, for truth is not an embellishment, but a wholeness. You have already discarded the shell and now you are presented with the actual fruit – the nut of which you are about to enjoy.

This life you have is a wondrous journey, the fullness of it immeasurable and you may enjoy all of those precious moments. You may feel sadness from time to time, about moments in the past, but you must not regret them, for they are all relevant to your life and to the lives of those with whom you had those encounters. It is as relevant to them as it has been to you.

<pre>
       Much concern is given
      To those deeds already done
            The recoil
         The letting of anger
         And limits that are set

            If all action
    Was given clearance by the mind
              Of purity
         Many of those ills
         Would be abandoned

           Though at times
    The mark of insanity may intervene
       By the mind that receives them
            In which case
       They are sick and need help
</pre>

The Importance of Words and Language

The people who were around when I was on your side of life had very little education, and we did not have a tenth of the words that you have now. Therefore, we wish to speak about communication, and of the way in which language and words have become so dominant. What I mean by this is that your language is changing all of the time. You are adopting new words and 'isms,' as of course did generations before you.

As we have continued to grow within the world of spirit, those of us who have wished to be of service to you have had to keep abreast of the manner of current language. So communication is not something you can fit into a given space, it is continual. Words are made up for new things, for new skills adopted and acquired and suchlike. As these new words are formulated, it makes sense that people begin to pick them up and use them in everyday language.

However, it seems to us that man is not able to pick up other facets of life, which are fundamentally basic, and that have remained basic and very real throughout eternity. It seems that certain facets of their lives are left disregarded on the quest for newer and brighter things, for longer and richer sentences, for words with new meaning.

An analogy could be made with science. After all, science creates half of the new words that exist within your sphere of life. Nevertheless, with all of this knowledge and accumulated wisdom, it seems that fundamental basics can be left on the top shelf gathering dust. Although there has been a wealth of knowledge accumulated throughout the years since spirit first communicated, the scientific world still refuses to accept the evidence of the continuity of life.

Yet, without accepting evidence and the possibility of new horizons, man could not have progressed to where he is now. He would still be using horse drawn carriages or still plowing and digging the fields as we did, gathering the harvest with hooks. You would not have your enormous machinery and clever ideas of communication. Of course, we applaud all of you, but you are still missing some basic information.

It must be partly down to a matter of whether you want to know something or not. You see, there is a difference just in those few words. For if you say that you believe in something, it is faith you are speaking of, and what we say is that we know … for faith has no place in real life.

Now, that may seem a little harsh, and I do not mean to split hairs about this. We are not trying to put those who have faith on one side of the fence and those who know on the other side. It is a matter of opinion. I suppose it is all about balance. You have to do both, for if you are to proceed and be the civilization that you wish to be, then you have to formulate choices of how, and for what benefit you may proceed.

I venture to say, as you increase your vocabulary, as you continue to grow with your learning, there are many things within the language you already have that can give you lights and pathways to the truth. In addition, there would be little point in we who have passed long before, in coming back to communicate with you, if we could not speak as you would understand. (Although, some on our side of life choose to come and speak in other languages or older languages, and this has its place too, for it broadens the mind.)

In your journey, think about how together we might derive some greater understanding. How we may receive more sincere depths of love and awareness from each other. We surely cannot strive to be content with ignorance. It is necessary for you to learn as much as you can in order to furnish those requirements. In order to ignite that spark within, so others may dwell in the fondness of knowledge and love.

Religion and Reincarnation

In your struggle to survive you all have an in-built wish to know more, and you may wonder at times just how you have made it this far, for you may have had very difficult lives. At least those of you, who are aware that there is a continuation in your survival, do not have quite the same worries as many of your fellow spirit travelers. You could say that these people are quite lucky really, in that they have an understanding of the truth. Such people will be aware that everything you do or say, your actions and every essence of being, is submitted for testament when you come to our side of life.

Humankind has created far too many problems and made the possibility of attainment of a higher nature much too difficult to reach. It is why very many people are now moving away from those religious doctrines, which are cumbersome, overbearing and immensely complicated, and have what we will call a 'sire' at the end of it. Likewise, for those who wish to follow gurus. Well-meaning folk who use word wisely, and yes, all are words of God this is true, but those who wish to encompass words spoken within a rigorous and stiff regime of indoctrination, are not wise.

I am not here to criticize or to pass judgment upon the wants and wishes of humankind; it is completely of your choice. You may walk along this path and feel you retain your higher self, but my friends, in spite of that which you follow, you would have done so anyway. It is not because of your involvement and entrenchment in that particular religion that has meant you have become a beautiful person. You were an aspect of God before you went there, even before you took those vows.

Words do not change a person. Deeds and thoughts in action are what change you. Thoughts are living things, and it is how you present yourself in life, in the day-to-day running of your lives, that count. There are all manner of people who would wish to run your life for you. There are plenty who will say the only way to God is to go to the 'big house' where God is. You must realize by now and having traveled the world in which you live, that this is not so.

There is not one person who is not worthy. There is not one soul who cannot come in. Nobody is singled out for punishment or negativity, for you will be your own judge. In the spirit side of life, my friends, all are equal. I say this in the most humble manner that I can, that I come to you in full face and honesty. I come to you always with love bound in love to give to you. To help you to realize the true extent of man's worth, to yourselves, and to each other – that is my pathway.

I would also have to say, there are many on your side of life, who feel that whatever they do they will be forgiven. Then there are others, who are so complacent, because they think they can come back again and have another go.

"Oh, its okay, I'll get it right next time!"

Now, I know these are all beliefs and this is one of the concepts of the human condition. Someone has an idea, and because all of the rest are lacking in any ideas and thoughts of their own, they adopt someone else's. That just because there are so many millions who also agree with it, it is felt it must be right. However, it is a strange paradox that one does not have a view of one's own – fathomed by one's own mind and understood by one's own receptors.

The mistake is made when they are all made to fit. Many facets of this religion or that religion, this doctrine or that, are taken upon oneself at will, other people's thoughts and ideas and not your own. So round and round in circles we go, until eventually, you find you are lost ... that you do not even have one original religion or concept.

Instead of getting an ice cream, you end up with an ice cube. It may have the same volume, but precious little in it. And so it goes on you see, for many believe whole-heartedly in what they hold to be right and true. Maybe some of it was true at a certain point in time, but perhaps it was written many years ago and was only applicable to that particular time.

This is not about religion. Spirit is not about religion. Spirit is about life – your inner-voice is about life. Many do not want to discuss spirit issues or even acknowledge the possibility, because of its association with death, and death is the darkest thing on man's mind. Most of your religious understandings talk of the afterlife, yet when presented with facts and issues relating to it, either deny its very existence, or claim license to bestow it. That it is only for those who adhere to certain rules and regulations, and so placing restrictions on who is worthy or not.

Therefore, you attempt to gain what understanding you have in accordance with your wish for survival; man's inherent wish for survival in-bred. Whilst the possibilities of 'maybe' and 'hope so' are like holding onto a piece of string whilst dangling over the edge of a cliff, when all you have is just the last little thread to hold onto. You have all of these minute little threads, where within your belief and understanding there is still doubt – for there is still fear of death. Still, fear that there will be an unknown. That there will be darkness or that there may be a horizon with a guru in the middle of it.

It is important that you understand, for your sanity and to make your life worthwhile, that you, at the end of your time within the physical world, will have done your best and tried to understand truly what life has to offer you. You can then take that understanding with you to the next stage in your journey of life.

Your existence upon the earth plane is a once only situation – it is not negotiable. Why would you want to keep coming back here? Do you think that the essence of your journey is fixed upon one place? Do you believe this is the only planet and universe or place where you can have a physical existence? Do you believe you would not be able to understand further information, further enlightenment of your mind and spirit if it were not for the world upon which you now inhabit? My friends, you have much more to look forward to other than these aspects of life that you endure now.

It is up to your free will to disseminate the fact from fiction, to understand where you are in the grand scheme of things. Then sometime later, you may look again and see how your understanding has improved and grown with your spirit light. Every moment of your existence, your spirit grows, even while you sleep; you do much work whilst you are asleep.

It is no great shame to discover the truth and admit it or to have a greater understanding and awareness of what you believe in. It is no great shame to be wrong, for to see that you are wrong is the first step to being right – the first step to your recovery.

We watch with love whilst we observe your progress and we know the love that you are grows with you day by day, on your journey of light.

Let us together
The spirit that I am
And my conscious physical being
Walk together within this journey
And think as one
How we may progress
Through communication
Love and understanding
And how we may benefit others
Who walk our walk
Within the power of love

Christmas

Christmas is the one time when many of your side of life are thinking of others, and we, in spirit, can do a great deal of good with the amount of love that is available then. We are able to do a vast amount of healing with it. As you may or may not be aware, those who are gravely ill around this time of year tend to come to our side of life, because the feeling of love is so heightened then.

I suppose it is a sad state of affairs that this emotion is so infrequent, but at least it gives mankind a chance to see and feel what it is like to give and receive love. A chance where each individual may move beyond the boundaries they have set themselves. You are raising your vibration when you give in a certain way, so imagine how different your side of life would be if you were not just doing it once a year. If you all gave more of your time to each other.

Showing that you care is not shedding emotion. It is not being weak or infantile. It is the act of wanting to give, to be of service. To be of help where it is needed. Even when it is not asked for ... to give help anyway.

Even in positions of care, where service is given to other people to produce a standard of living, it is still the act of giving to another human being, to another spirit. Even here, there are those who give this grudgingly, but admittedly, friends, true service largely goes unnoticed to most upon your side of life. However, the individual who is truly giving, who is sharing the cup of love from within, knows it is a pleasure not often found.

If only man could grow to understand the pleasure involved in giving, of giving love freely without any wish for return. Yes, indeed, this would improve the lot of the human spirit greatly, as well as man the animal, for in true nature it would manifest as a knock-on effect towards the rest of your environment. Just by caring – just by showing love.

Therefore, we, on the spirit side, do relish Christmas time, and it is why it is the time of light – the festival of light. Though not just in a singular religious sense. Not just for the specific Christian belief perhaps, but because across your realm it is a time for giving and receiving.

Unfortunately, this celebration has become far too preoccupied with materialism, and one day, perhaps those on your side will shed these unwanted clothes and adorn themselves with a more genuine approach to their life and the life of their offspring.

What this instills is not the thought behind the act of giving or receiving; it is instilling the act of 'I want' and I get what 'I want.'

'I want,' only really ends up with negative waste, for 'I want,' does not receive what they deserve, but what they think they are due.

In reality, what happens is that humankind is never satisfied; the hole is never filled, for the 'I want' somehow never satisfies the need or the greed and becomes blank and

Christmas

meaningless. Such is the product of life friends.

I hope that in time, man might perceive something other than what they expect, but it is difficult when they just give material gifts intended to fill material needs. Not only are they empty, but before your life is through they are useless. What you were given just a few years ago is now out of fashion, out of date or broken. On the other hand, maybe you have simply lost interest, for it does not hold the same benefit to you that it did. Your life has moved on and you now have new wants and needs. New desires and new lists of shopping that you would wish to have.

However, love is not like that. Love is pure and you can never get enough of it, yet it fills you up to the brim. The gift of love to each other is unrivalled. As we give to each other, we grow in the bountiful gifts we are able to bestow with free will and full meaning.

All spirit love is generous – generous to the point of bursting. It has no boundaries, knows no color. It does not realize ugliness or poverty, but opens doors to the world of eternal life. The knowing that is deep within you and the upliftment you receive by giving is reward enough. Just to see that love has come to stay upon the lips, mind, and heart of every fellow traveler you meet. Every single individual is worthy ... every single one unique.

The life that you have now is just a mere excerpt of the life that you are having and will continue to have. It is like looking at a comma on a page in a book and thinking of all the reasons why that comma should be there.

Well, your time upon your side of life now, is like a comma within a sentence, within a paragraph, within a chapter, within a book.

There is so much more for you to discover, so we say 'happy days,' and may God, as you understand it, always be with you.

By what we serve up in cups of thought
We pour out and call by another name
We take what we need from it
Then perhaps dish it out in another way
Forgetting the containment it had

Remember thoughts are living things
And take more care of them
For they may bless us
They may place our next step
Upon the road of freedom

Sitting and Frustration

We come from spirit with love, through the universal energy that allows us all to exist. Of course, without it nothing would exist, and you cannot have nothing. There always has to be something – whether you see it or not. There is always something right in front of you. It may be gases, microorganisms, or things you plainly see. It could be any of a number of your friends from the spirit side of life, who regularly come and join you. Here they can stand before you, and you can either be aware or be completely unaware of their presence, or even their existence.

Whether sitting in meditation for your own spirit development or for the development of interaction with we, on our side, remember, it is the interaction with your self that is ultimately so important. As we have mentioned many times, there just does not appear to be the words in your vocabulary or within our recollections of words, of how we can explain or describe to you certain elements of energy and vibration that only exist in our realm.

In order to do this sort of work, we have to do much studying and continue all the while in trying to improve our communication. Sometimes, we have lapses and sometimes you also have lapses, and it can be so difficult to get it right, to bring our vibrations together. Occasionally, even though you may sense our vibration close to you, you cannot seem to get the connection, and yet at other times, it can seem so easy.

We do understand your frustration, but never fear we are always with you; we can see you too. To our side of life you can appear as reflected images, as light, vibration, color, or mist. You do not realize the efforts we make in our realm. You may not feel that anything is happening, but we are helping you to build various filters within your auric field, within your psyche, within your whole being. Auric filters, vibrational filters, color filters and filters of sound, so that you may not only sense thought and feeling, but acknowledge it within your realm.

It will always be different because all communicators are different, as are all of you – for you are all individual. Therefore, in your meditation, if you can be peaceful and trusting, relaxed, and focused on nothing at all in particular, we can broaden certain aspects, and help with how and in which ways, you may develop the gifts you have. How you may wish to improve yourself is of course your free will, it is your choice and destiny to measure to within the being of light that you are.

We, in spirit, are always trying new things, so they can be new experiences for us both. Consequently, even though you may feel that your progress may be slow, it is not. For every uneventful moment that seems to pass you by, just think of how many moments there actually are in your life, and you are only observing a fraction. Think of all of those other moments that may have been swept under the carpet or have been in the backwater of your life,

Sitting and Frustration

and all of those moments yet to come. Each one can be an illumination to you. Each one can have a character all of its own.

We understand how frustrating it must be for you at times, when you are perhaps unable to sense spirit or grasp what we try to bring you. That you may be aware of all of these things, yet you cannot see them or touch them, or do anything about it. Do not despair – for truly, you will be moving forward, and each moment is a delight to behold and savor.

If you feel the pull and push
Of how obstinate
The lack of control
Of your own mind can become
Think for a moment
Upon those who walk your walk
Who have no control
On those thoughts that come

If all could acknowledge
And befriend those thoughts
Who come from far off places
Perhaps they would be brighter
Happier beings
In receiving them

Guide Hierarchy

For many, when you are establishing yourselves within the seeking and acknowledgement of we, in the spirit world, there appears to have arisen some form of hierarchy.

Some form of: "I have a better guide than your guide." Or: "My spirit helpers are doctors and philosophers who were important historical figures, so I must be a far more worthy channel than you to attract such individuals."

It is a total mystery to us how man seeks to benefit the spirit world, but seems to conclude that the benefit and reward must be higher with a soul of higher learning from past earth history. Then there are those who were already in spirit when they became of note: Silver Birch perhaps, or White Eagle. There are even those on your side of life who claim to have them!

It's almost as if one would wish to pull one's hair out. That they have missed the point again. That there has to be jostling for higher positions, for ladies and gentlemen of high regard. If we are to answer and search truthfully for what we know to exist, it does not matter who becomes the communicator. It can be Winston Churchill, or it can be Robert Jones from number 29, upper something street.

It should not be about the perceived depth of the spirit communicator by their name, but concerning that, which is spoken, surely. It is that, which is felt within the breast, in the way your heart races at the message, the sounds and syllables, and the love that permeates through the voice.

It almost seems that the more one is patted upon the back, the more that ridiculousness between the human race survives; the weighing up of good deeds on the one hand, with the ridicule of intelligence on the other. Or so-called, because civilization, as you understand it, barely holds a thimble full of what intelligence really is, then says this is the highest point that we can get to.

Do you see, that in order to be intellectually boastful and have prowess in a given area, you need to have many supporting pieces of paper and adulation of other civilized members of your society. Yet, there are so many pure individuals who seek to blend within their surroundings, within the spirit that they are, whether they are aware of spirit guides or not. They blend and give love in service to others, and have maybe awakened far more facets and assets of the personality of their spirit. A combination of the mental mind of matter with the spiritual mind and they have found there is a union that works.

The journey of light is long and bounteous. It is not perfect, for you are not perfect and I am not perfect. We all seek to acquire greater understanding, higher characteristics of a beneficial spirit, and not for ourselves, but to aid each other. In so seeking that benefit, we can then accumulate a greater depth of understanding of each other's wants and needs. Of each other's desires of love and friendship, and the abhorrence at horrors and deficit of negativity.

It is all to humanity's advantage that communications between us should survive, and we should all encourage each other. Not by whom we are working with, but with what we can give to each other; how we may perpetrate a greater understanding and love.

You are in true service
When in the act of giving out
You are not thinking
About what effect
Your personality
Is going to gain
From doing so

If you are not thinking
Of how others may see you
You are living

It is the moment
When you are thinking
Of how others may see you
That you cease to be you
As you are consciously
Making an effort
To be someone
You are not

Spirit and Other Life

I do not think you quite understand how privileged we feel at being able to make this journey within the realms of light and love. We are given to the service of all our brothers and sisters, within the spirit light and on your side of life, and we do so with eagerness and in anticipation of each moment. We travel within the bounds and energies of love itself – the universal energy that enables all life to exist. Not just you upon the physical plane or we, in the spirit, but all life, within all of the spirit realms known and unknown. To all sides of the universe and other universes not yet even perceived by ourselves.

Within your realm, there are many, many life forms of which you are unaware, many other beings elsewhere within your galaxies. These may exist at the same time and space, but could also be a lot further away. There are other beings within your time frame within your physical existence, and the fact that you have not found them yet, is immaterial.

Perhaps they do not wish to be found. They may just be wholesome beings living a peaceful life, not wishing to be interrupted. They may actually be as unaware of you as you are of them, but it does not mean to say they do not exist.

Look at it this way. You know for a fact that there are very many people living in other parts of the world, but you do not have to go there in order to believe it. You see snapshots of instances, keyholes of life from anywhere on your planet on a regular basis. You acknowledge them and know they are there, because you have seen them. And this is exactly the same analogy with the spirit side of life in relation to your plane of existence. Just because people on your side are unaware or ignorant of the facts, it does not mean to say that we are just idealistic fabrics of your fertile imagination.

Of course not, and I suppose you could say: "Well why do you keep us all in ignorance for so long, if it is so simple? Why does the spirit side of life not just materialize and say hello?"

It is not as simplistic as that and it would not work if presented in that way. If all of mankind were aware of their true nature at once, how would they learn? How would you be able to move forward? Everything would stop, because you are of the nature of taking and commanding, moving only for profit and gain. How would you ever learn about how you might give, if it is all just presented on a plate?

Can you imagine: "Do not worry about that friend – you live forever anyway!" There would be mayhem and total lack of care.

Additionally, in the case of the life forms from other realms, well – in this instance, mankind may not embrace every facet of existence, for you are much too dangerous and cannot be trusted in your present climate of mind. And this is not a judgment, it is a truth. It is just that you have not learnt yet. The more that mankind dreams and wishes for command of every aspect of life, so the more it will be taken away, for you as a human race will not ever move forward with this outlook.

However, for those upon your side of life who are ready for the experience, who are serious and ready to take the challenges, understanding may be given and received. Not made in haste or by some whimsical judgment, but in deed, contemplation, and earnest work. As we have said before, you do not have to be a master of the universe to understand the concept and the realities of life. You can be just a simple soul, and this is why it applies equally to everyone, to understand and communicate the ever-loving aspect of God, which is a part of us all. We are the same. We are just in different modes, different structures, within different frames of reference.

As the mind expands with knowledge
We call thoughts and ask them in
Saying all the time
We will give them a good home

There is plenty of room within the spirit
If the thoughts you have are positive, good and whole
If your thoughts are caring
Then they do not have to be held within

Because of their purity they may be let free
To travel and land upon some other unsuspecting spirit
And give them a chance to smile
And remark upon their energy and finer light

For Those Walking the Spirit Path

Some souls on your side would say that our influence upon your state of mind and well-being is detrimental to your progress of life. Some would say many untruths in order to shame or discredit those of you who are involved within spirit work. Even though they may have many credentials, all of that knowledge and wisdom they claim to have stored inside counts for nothing, if they rely upon text written. It all counts for nothing friend, if the truth cannot be seen for what it is.

If you rely on analysis of first impressions, no matter how hard anyone tries to discredit it, because of strength and conviction, you will just continue to move forward. You will be unwavering and undaunted by those tasks and mountains you have to climb – the mountain of ignorance, prejudice, and self-worth.

This is indeed a tough road. It is not easy to lay your fears to one side, and it is no mean task to put down your spear. Often, it may seem as though you have to, in some way, accept attack as being part of the human response to your existence.

It can leave one feeling a little despondent, knowing that so many people on your side of life are so devoid of knowledge of their spirit. That many do not wish to know or just refuse to know. That you yourself make all of this effort, searching and listening, stretching all your senses, raising yourself and your awareness, and you simply cannot understand why others do not see it, feel it, or want to. To some extent, there is nothing you can do to help them to discover their own light, unless they wish to do so.

It doesn't take a lot I agree, not really in the general scheme of things. Nevertheless, to some it is an awesome and tiresome subject, for it involves God and anything to do with God does not go down well with the tea and biscuits!

Many may think in this way because of a past negative experience, or they may perceive God as a wizened old man in flowing robes, with a long white beard. It is only because of their limited vision that they cannot see anything else. They maybe do not wish to – but they are not a lost cause or an effect that you must ignore.

As long as you shine your light and you communicate with your spirit, then by those lessons given, people around you with whom you interact, will begin to see what drives you.

Yes, they may well be aggravated at some points of disagreement, and they may possibly try to be humiliating even. However, as your life progresses and your love and fulfillment overflows, your light shines out before you and they will know deep within themselves of your discovery. Their fruit will be delivered unto them in the fullness of time. As more and more experiences are related through the voice, through media and through vision, they will see that there is undeniable proof, if they would just take the trouble to look.

For Those Walking the Spirit Path

Many do not even notice the beauty of your world; they do not see the proof of God's love, which is all around. Many regard it as something to just walk on, as something to stand upon to look elsewhere and may still only see a solitary figure in the distance walking towards them. Your planet is not as empty as it appears and there is so much more for you to take in. Your life is a golden journey; not of reverence or platitudes to higher beings, but within your own right, through your will and through the love that you can generate.

You may seek the wisdom of the higher mind, of the higher intelligence from within and without this universe and others. You owe it to yourself and everyone you meet, to go within, to go with these positive harnesses to aid you. When you meditate, you sit with your inner voice; try to recognize every emotion, everything that is spoken softly from within. It is natural, and once you have discarded your fears, your presence will grow even greater.

Take courage and strength in your learning process as you move forward. Let your spirit guide you … always the next chapter will come, in your never-ending story of life.

The Keys

You have two keys with which to enhance your life. The first key unlocks the inside door, the door to the spirit within – the door that shows you the way to find yourself. Each moment is precious, so you must make the time to sit for yourself; even ten to twenty minutes a day, to reach that golden place within – that place where the real you resides.

The second is the key to access, the key that opens the outside door – the door to the great world that surrounds you. So there are two keys. One is to your inner door and the other key is to your outer door. You see, you have been living in your 'house' all this time, and you did not have any keys!

These two keys are vital for your enhancement and unfoldment so do not forget them, for with practice they will teach you much about the individual that you are. They are necessary to your life, because through them you may unfold your journey, to follow your true destiny.

They enable you to unlock the doors of the reality that exists for you. To lead you into a new expansion of your mind, with a wonderful openness with the spirit that you are. They will help you to move forward in greater trust and harmony, and perhaps make you aware of the actual disharmony that you live in.

Once you have really attained harmony, you will truly never wish for anything else other than to blend with the universal flux of life, and with the ebb and flow of energy between the physical plane and the spirit ... because it is all one.

It is good to have the keys to your own home so you may come and go as you wish. So that you may relax into the life, you have made for yourself.

Meditation
The Master Key

In order to find direction, one must first of all find the initial signpost. Firstly, look for a quiet place, the quieter the better, although this is not essential, it does help. After having found this place of quiet, it is advisable to begin to wind down some little time before the event if possible, so that the matters of the physical world in which you live can start to dissipate from your mind. This would be a standard practice for any meditation.

Always open with an invocation or prayer asking for protection of spirit, to illumine the love within you and for you to become accustomed with your natural and rightful birthright as a fellow spirit traveler who is having a human experience.

In the beginning, the sitter should be comfortable and learn firstly to still the mind. This may seem an impossible task to some, or probably to many.

There are various mechanisms for being able to go within and be silent, but we suggest that if any thoughts come into your mind, just allow them to and then let them go again. Just accept them, but do not take too much notice. You will soon learn to pay them less attention and perhaps stop them in their tracks altogether in the fullness of time and with practice.

You will find that over a period of time, the thoughts that come in from the physical world will be less and less. When you first try, you may not get what you think you should be getting, but what you should get – is nothing. Then as you look within (as opposed to looking outside of yourself) very slowly and gently, certain pictures or ideas may become evident within your mind; you will also feel an awareness of new feelings. Gradually, you will find that perhaps colors or sensations about your body will occur. When this happens, learn to breathe gently, rhythmically, and relax. If you stop and think too much about it, your inquisitive mind will want to 'open the box' – try not to be tempted to do this.

You will find friends, that as you open up more and more to this way of being, to the light and the warmth within, the spirit that you are will become unfolded, and your thoughts will expand before your very eyes and within your mind. You will then be able to take on board new understanding and new meaning, for you will see that the world is not as you thought it was. It is blessed, gentle, and loving towards every one of you.

You can learn to relax within this vibration and learn to raise the vibration of life that is within you. Do not sit in meditation for too long at first, 20 minutes is sufficient, but try to allot some time in your day when you may do this. Finish each meditation with a closing prayer or invocation. Always think with utmost peace, love, and harmony, during these times, and perhaps it will begin to change your life. In fact, I know it will!

As you move from one moment of understanding to another and enlighten to the love that is not only within you, but surrounds you, then you will know … life is eternal!

Eternal Spirit
Dear Father, Mother, Creator, Friend
Help me to release my spirit
To feel how it may soar
Above the clouds
Of delusion and clamor
That we may all see
And define our route
Our journey of greater haste
For the benefit we make
Is for all

May love and peace
Always be the stride you make
To journey for benefit
Help and happiness
May 'Lord Is'
Always bless every move
And motivation
Behind your inner most thoughts
And actions
That they be the right ones
To shine in love

Gregory Haye